The Architecture of
the Monastic Library in Italy
1300-1600

Antonello da Messina, *St. Jerome in His Study, ca.* 1470 (reproduced by courtesy of the Trustees, The National Gallery, London).

JAMES F. O'GORMAN

The Architecture of the Monastic Library in Italy 1300-1600

Catalogue with Introductory Essay

PUBLISHED BY

NEW YORK UNIVERSITY PRESS

for the College Art Association of America

NEW YORK 1972

Monographs on Archaeology and the Fine Arts
sponsored by
THE ARCHAEOLOGICAL INSTITUTE OF AMERICA
and
THE COLLEGE ART ASSOCIATION OF AMERICA
XXV
Editor: Lucy Sandler

Alla mia cara
e
ai miei cari

Acknowledgments

This publication grows out of my doctoral dissertation (Harvard, 1966), written under the aegis of James S. Ackerman to whom I am indebted for continued encouragement. For contributions, assistance, and/or discussion on this side of the Atlantic, I want to acknowledge Richard Betts, Gino Corti, Charles Dempsey, Samuel Edgerton, Walter Gibson, Rab Hatfield, Naomi Miller, David M. Robb, Cervin Robinson, Charles Stuckey, and especially, Rudolf Hirsch. While publicly thanking them for their help, I accept full responsibility for all conclusions. Finally, my wife deserves particular mention for many photographs, and more patience.

In Italy I received help and hospitality from the following individuals: Dottore Emanuele Casamassima (Florence), Dottore Giovanni Cecchini (Perugia), Professore Luigi Crema (Milan), Padre Ludovico Maschietto, O.S.B. (Padua), Padre Ambrogio Montani, O.S.B. (Parma), Dottore Guido Morozzi (Florence), Professore Giulio Muratori (Ferrara), Conte Emilio Nasali-Rocca (Piacenza), Dottoresse Laura Oliva (Crema), the late Padre Stefano Orlandi, O.P. (Florence), Professore Lionello Puppi (Padua), Padre Stefano Rabacchi, O.P. (Bologna), Signora Laura Tanini (Badia a Settimo), Dottore Sergio Zanarotti (Vicenza), and many other unnamed monks, soldiers, doctors, scholars, and civil servants from Rome to Milan and Venice. *A tutti i miei più vivi ringraziamenti!*

In Rome I was permitted the resources of the American Academy, the Biblioteca Hertziana, the Istituto Storico Germanico, and the Istituto Nazionale di Archeologia e Storia dell'Arte. In Florence I used the Biblioteca Nazionale Centrale, and the ample library of the Kunsthistorisches Institut. The dissertation was written in March, 1966, in the Chalet of the Villa La Torrossa in Fiesole; revised and amplified in Philadelphia, 1967-70.

J. F. O'G.

Merion Station, Pennsylvania
Spring, 1971

Preface

THE HISTORY OF ARCHITECTURE in Renaissance Italy has traditionally been written from the formal evidence that can be derived from studying three building types: church, palace, and villa. But church, palace, and villa represent only a portion of Renaissance culture, which also created the need for other building types: the monastery, the hospital, educational buildings, and so on, all of which have been too little studied. It will become clear in the course of the following essay that the library, a part of the monastic complex, although not as frequent a commission as the church or palace, cannot be overlooked if we want a broad understanding of the Renaissance and its architecture. Vespasiano da Bisticci, the fifteenth-century Florentine bookseller, tells us that Pope Nicholas V (1447-1455) "used to say that he would do two things if ever he had the money: collect books and erect buildings. And in his papacy he did both." [1] The monastic library marked the confluence of these two Renaissance passions, architecture and learning, and was therefore a most important architectural problem. By examining this building type as the response to specific and general problems of need and use, as well as of form, my intention is not to alter the traditional view of architecture in Renaissance Italy, but to supplement and enrich it.

The building type discussed here is the monastic room housing a communal reference library, or noncirculating collection of manuscript books. The study is limited to monastic libraries because in the fifteenth and sixteenth centuries in Italy, as earlier, the most important collections of books—other than those possessed by a few rich princes, and that in the Vatican—were deposited in monastic establishments. In the following essay we shall see why.

This study is intended to be suggestive rather than definitive. A definitive study of the monastic library in Renaissance Italy, and the larger problem of the architecture of the Renaissance monastery as a whole, must await the thorough investigation of the records of suppressed monasteries now preserved in the many State Archives of Italy, which would be a lifetime task. And the complete examination of the many existing but frequently inaccessible fifteenth- and sixteenth-century monasteries has scarcely been begun. The few libraries discussed here are only the published remnants of the great number that must have been erected in Italy from the fourteenth through the sixteenth centuries. Time has taken a heavy toll of these as of all monastic buildings. Some fifteenth-century libraries, such as that attributed to Michelozzo at S. Giorgio Maggiore in Venice (Cat. 52), succumbed to Baroque rebuilding, but many probably fell victim to suppression by secular authorities of religious institutions in Italy during the late eighteenth and nineteenth centuries. From the point of view of architectural preservation, the occupation of the peninsula by Napoleon was disastrous.[2] During the time of the Jacobin Republic of Rome alone, a list of houses suppressed under the laws of 1798 numbers some 309 monasteries and 32 nunneries, and this list is incomplete![3] Many suppressed houses were returned to their orders after Napoleon's fall, only to be closed again at the Unification in the 1860s. Some more were returned to the religious at the Conciliation of 1929. Not all possessed great libraries, and not all the secularized monasteries have been totally destroyed. A monastery could be converted easily into a military barracks (Cat. 37), a school (Cat. 9), a museum (Cat. 37), or a hospital (Cat. 47), and such a conversion usually meant the building would have to be remodelled somewhat. Concerning libraries, suppression meant the books would be removed to public depositories, and the library furnishings destroyed as well. That is, the suppressed monasteries were denuded of their books and furnishings and their libraries altered beyond recognition. So, people forgot for more than a century and a half that many of these rooms had been used for libraries. Some have come to be recognized for what they were originally only as recently as the post-World War II period (Cat. 45), when military establishments in Italy were reconverted to other uses. No doubt there are more still unrecognized in *carabinieri* barracks and like establishments that are off limits to the *forestiere* unless he has very good luck, much time, great patience, and an extraordinary ability to cut red tape.

The study of library buildings can be aided by documents, both visual and verbal, but here too the lacunae are large. Old exterior views of such libraries as those at S. Giorgio Maggiore in Venice (Fig. 58) or S. Croce in Florence (Fig. 32) force us to speculate about their interior design. What I believe is the contemporary representation of the interior of a monastic library does appear in the right background of Antonello da Messina's *St. Jerome in His Study* (*ca.* 1470), but it is recognizable as such only because it resembles basilical spaces (Frontispiece). This recognition may help us understand Antonello's enigmatic painting,[4] but it adds little to the history of the fifteenth-century monastic library. The remarkable documentation preserved for the libraries at SS. Annunziata in Florence (Cat. 19), the Laurentian in Florence (Cat. 22), S. Sepolcro in Piacenza (Cat. 47), or S. Agostino in Cremona (Cat. 14) is at present very rare, although it will certainly be supplemented by continued archival research.

There is one kind of written source—the library inventory—that is available for a large number of libraries because students of intellectual history have long been interested in the contents of medieval and Renaissance libraries. These inventories often provide information of architectural significance. Indeed, for the period before 1400 they are our only sources, because very few trecento monastic libraries have survived in Italy, and to my knowledge none remains intact. These inventories often provide our only clue to the original appearance of a lost or altered library (Cat. 48), and can augment our knowledge of an existing one that has lost its original books and furnishings (Cat. 21). Inventories are of importance second only to the buildings themselves in the study of the monastic library in Italy.

The lack of complete information precludes the possibility of a definitive study now, and the introductory essay, devoted to the architectural history (in the broadest sense) of the monastic library, is accordingly speculative. Especially in the early parts where I have gone far beyond the confines of my own professional competence, historians of cultural and religious history may find the discussion at best superficial. But that is a necessary risk. I have also dared to take a generalized rather than a particularized approach to deal with a group of works located in a large geographical area rather than minutely documenting one or more works in one locale. In this spirit too, I have collected under the name "monastery" all communal religious houses, whether they were, in fact, monasteries, friaries, or canonries. The need to consider monastic libraries built over a broad span of time, indicated by the title, will become apparent in the course of the essay. Any less-inclusive approach would have obscured my main objective, which is to provide working generalizations concerning the construction of these buildings and a list of references in the catalogue (in which are gathered a fortuitous collection of data about extant and lost libraries), hopefully to encourage further study and discussion of a neglected chapter in Renaissance life and art.

If the working generalizations presented here one day seem unsound, and the material covered in the catalogue incomplete, the research and discussion required to demonstrate such conclusions will have justified this publication. The pioneer expects that the cultivation of settlers will change the shape of his clearing.[5]

Contents

List of Illustrations

I Introductory Essay

THE MALATESTIANA

CESENA IS A SMALL, noisy town near the lower end of the Via Emilia, that slanting aorta of the Province of Emilia-Romagna joining Rimini on the Adriatic coast to Piacenza on the Lombard border. The center of town is the present Piazza Bufalini, defined on the north by the drab yellow stucco front of the Biblioteca Malatestiana. Behind this later facade stands one of the most engaging interior spaces in Italy, indeed, in Europe (Figure 24). The physical and historical core of the Biblioteca Malatestiana is the room and the collection of manuscripts that originally formed part of the local Franciscan house (Cat. 11). Erected between 1447 and 1452 by Matteo Nuti for the local tyrant, Malatesta Novello, brother of the more famous Sigismondo Malatesta of Rimini, the Malatestiana is unique among Italian libraries erected before 1500 because it alone retains its original furnishings and manuscripts. Only here can we grasp as a totality the architecture of a monastery library in quattrocento Italy.

The original Franciscan library is a long narrow room located on the upper level of a two-story brick building that once formed a central wing of the destroyed monastery (Figs. 14B, 24-28). The floor of the library is sustained by cross-vaults resting upon the lower outer walls and a central row of piers that divide the ground floor into two aisles. The library above is also vaulted, but its vaults rest upon brick half-columns engaged to the outer walls, and two rows of free-standing fluted columns with curious capitals bearing heraldic devices (Fig. 24). These upper vaults are restrained by tie rods and surmounted by massive wood trusses that form a gable roof (Fig. 25).

1

The space within is articulated: the free-standing columns divide the room into three aisles. It is a "basilical" space, and the central aisle, covered with a barrel vault, is narrower than the cross-vaulted side aisles. Reading desks are located in the side aisles (Fig. 27), and the manuscripts are chained to a rod running the length of the shelf built into the desk on which they are stored flat. Above this shelf is a sloping surface upon which a volume is placed while it is read. The central aisle forms the major passageway between these reading desks, and there are minor passageways as well between the desks and the side walls.

The room is entered from one end through a rather squat, pedimented doorway surmounted by elephants symbolic of the Malatesta clan. From the entrance the visitor looks down the central passageway flanked by columns and surmounted by a continuous barrel vault that races away from him toward the far end of the room (Fig. 24). The room is illuminated by the series of relatively small but numerous windows that break the warm green, stuccoed surface of the long side walls. These windows admit a soft, symmetrical light that suffuses the space but only slightly illuminates it. The library must always have struck the visitor as a long, low, vaulted, divided, twilight tunnel.

The tourist can enjoy these characteristics of the Biblioteca Malatestiana without further ado, but the historian asks himself what this room has to tell him about late medieval learning and architecture, and where it stands in relation to other rooms of like use. The following essay proposes some answers to these questions.

MONASTERY AND SCHOOL

The builders of the monastic libraries in Renaissance Italy continued, with modifications, in the tradition of the late medieval type, for the large monastic communal reference library was first created around 1300. As we shall see, it was developed to fulfill the shared requirements of two of the most important medieval institutions: Monasticism, renewed by the advent of the friars in the early thirteenth century, and the University, which can be traced back before the twelfth century.

The early medieval monastery housed the Benedictine Order and its many off-shoots. It was typically rural and typically self-sufficient. It was a small city, and within its walls most aspects of medieval life and industry could be carried out. The famous ninth-century plan for a monastery from the library at St. Gall in Switzerland shows the church as the most important element in the layout. It is surrounded by other structures that contain the entire spectrum of daily activities;

living quarters for the monks, breweries, bakeries, a coopery, stables, gardens, infirmaries, barns, shops, areas for animals, a mill, and a press, among others (Fig. 1).

The monks were expected to lead a quotidian life of transcendental prayer and physical toil. They were also expected to read. But the fact that they became the means by which the learning of the ancient world was transferred to us—the romance of their miraculous achievement—has I think produced an exaggerated notion about the size of the book collections within these early medieval monastic establishments. They were smaller than might be imagined. For example, the average size of 21 monastic collections dating from the eighth to the twelfth century, listed by Gustav Becker in his *Catalogi bibliothecarum antiqui,* is much less than 300 volumes.[6] The largest collection, at Bobbio in the tenth century, contained 666 volumes. Such figures may actually represent more works, of course, since more than one work might be bound into one volume, but the architectural historian, as opposed to the intellectual historian, is primarily interested in the bulk of such collections rather than their literary content. His task is to determine how the books were stored. As we shall see, before around 1300, how these manuscripts were stored was of very little architectural interest.

The St. Gall exemplar places the library on the floor above the scriptorium, itself occupying a small square room to the left of the main apse of the church.[7] Its location suggests that this library was intended to house the books used in the church service, but even so the library indicated in this scheme was probably of exceptional dimensions. It is more characteristic that it had little physical identity of its own; this was also true of the typical Cistercian layout. As a monk moved into the church from the monastery at Fossanova, a late twelfth-century abbey near Rome, he passed an ambry set into the cloister wall just to the right of the entrance (Fig. 2). This ambry, or *armarium* in Latin, served as the library.[8] Here the monk picked up the book he would need during the divine office in the church. Any other reading—and we must think in terms of one or two books a year, and not misjudge the early Middle Ages by our own voracious appetite for reading matter [9]—was done in the seclusion of the monk's cell or while he walked in the cloister arcades. Books for this purpose were distributed from a storage vault, or book room, often placed next to the sacristy. The book room at Fossanova is a windowless space 10 by 14 feet, and that is scarcely large enough to generate much architectural excitement.

These few examples are cited to illustrate the main characteristic of the early medieval monastic library. It was architecturally insignificant because it was rarely more than a mere storage vault.[10] The conception of the library as an ideal environment for the storage *and* study of manuscripts, as a place set aside for human scholarly activity, appears later.

As we have seen, such a library room had been built at Cesena in the middle of the fifteenth century, but this was not the first or most dramatic. The library in the Dominican friary of S. Marco in Florence (Cat. 23) was constructed when the convent was rebuilt after 1438, presumably from the designs of Michelozzo. The view of the monastery from the north-east that appears at the foot of the *Crucifixion*, a fresco by Giovanni Antonio Sogliani dated 1536 and located on the end wall of the main refectory of this same monastery, shows the church to the right, from the rear, and the library to the left (Fig. 42). The library now rivals the church as the architectural focus of the entire monastic complex. The plan of this monastery demonstrates that the variety of activities represented in the earlier rural monasteries has now disappeared (Figs. 39-40). It has become a specialized institution. It is no longer rural, but urban; it is no longer a complex organism, but a relatively simple one. The requirements of the church and the devotions contained within it are still the primary considerations for the spatial development of the monastery, but, outside of the church, there is just one other main concern: study. The monastery now houses a world devoted exclusively to prayer and to learning, so its parts have been reduced to church and chapter room, dormitories and refectories, cloisters, and the communal reference library (Fig. 38). The latter is no longer an insignificant area as it is in the St. Gall exemplar. In plan, internal spatial organization, and external mass, it has become one of the most important parts of the architectural complex. In fact it is second only to the church itself.

In size and importance the rooms at Florence and Cesena are typical of the monastic libraries of the fifteenth century in Italy, but rooms that served to store a large reference collection within an urban monastery can be traced back into the mid-thirteenth century, but no farther. About 1270 the Dominican Humbertus de Romanus recommended the formation of a reference collection in which well-written volumes would be chained to reading desks for frequent use by the friars in a suitable and quiet place within the monastery.[11] It will become clear later that Humbertus's advice was followed from about 1300 onward not only by his own Preachers but by the other orders as well. The rooms constructed to house these reference collections mark the origin of post-classical library architecture, because in them the housing of books for the convenience of scholars became a large-scale architectural problem for the first time since classical antiquity. The history of modern library architecture begins in the late thirteenth century.

Humbertus based his advice on meeting the broader social and institutional needs that grew out of certain thirteenth-century historical developments. The communities of men gathered together under the Rules of St. Dominic (d. 1221) and St. Francis (d. 1226), as well as the lesser mendicant Orders (the Austin Hermits, the Carmelites) that arose in the thirteenth century, were primarily dedicated to teaching. The earlier monks were usually shut up within their city-like complexes; the friars studied within the monastery in order to preach outside of it. For the latter learning was a tool. The Dominicans, founded specifically to combat heresy, recognized from the beginning the need for an intellectual arsenal, but even the Franciscans, founded by a man opposed to learning because he believed the ideal friar would be *idiota,* very early became a studious Order including within its ranks such learned men as Bonaventure and Bacon. These mendicant Orders grew into educational systems. Monastic education was achieved within the monastic structure; the monastery became a school.[12] Local schools fed provincial schools, which in turn fed the *studia generalia,* or university level monastic schools, usually located in an urban center. These monasteries were urban rather than rural, like the older monasteries, because they were consciously located in those cities that possessed a secular *studium,* or university. In such centers the friars could take advantage of the resources of an educational system of recognized learning and great prestige that already was well established.[13] Thus, it comes as no surprise to learn that the headquarters of the Dominican Order was established in Bologna (Cat. 2), the location of one of the oldest and most important universities of the Middle Ages, or that the Franciscans, whose mother house was understandably in Assisi, early founded a *studium generale* in theology at S. Francesco in Bologna (Cat. 3). But the friars in Italy were not mere leeches; they made their own contribution in this juxtaposition of monastery and school.

The primary function of the monastic library as it developed in the late thirteenth century was to serve the needs of students within the monastic educational system, which explains the presence of large libraries even in cities, such as Milan, that never possessed a university, but I would also like to suggest that they filled an even broader role, what might be called their "public" function (in a very restricted sense), for those libraries in monasteries adjacent to urban universities.

Hastings Rashdall lists major Italian universities in Turin, Pavia, Piacenza, Verona, Padua, Modena, Ferrara, Bologna, Pisa, Florence (intermittently), Siena, Perugia, Rome, and Naples at the end of the fourteenth century.[14] Because Bologna was the oldest and most important, and in many ways the model for all other Italian universities, and even more because we are well supplied with studies of all aspects of its history, it will be the focus of our attention here.

The origins of the Bolognese university can be traced beyond the twelfth century and yet, with the possible exception of the Spanish College, erected between 1365 and 1367 by provision of the will of Cardinal Albornoz to accommodate just 24 poor Iberian students at the *studium,* the first building designed and constructed to house the school at Bologna was the Archiginnasio, erected between 1561 and 1563. Perhaps Bologna was late in providing its school with a building of its own, but not as late as might be imagined, for few other Italian medieval *studia* to my knowledge received specifically designed homes before the late fifteenth century.[15] There was a temporal gap of at least three centuries in which this important institution was without architectural definition, and in the case of Bologna that period was stretched to four centuries. Not until the Renaissance was this medieval institution made architecturally manifest.

Pearl Kibre has summed up this situation beautifully in the opening sentence of her study of the medieval nations.[16] "The medieval university had reference not to a handsome campus nor to venerable old buildings," she began, "but rather to the society of scholars and students who gathered in a particular place, the *studium.*" In an era like ours, when buildings have been erected before there existed an adequately defined function which they were to serve, when that is, the image precedes the act, the fact that an institution as large as the medieval university might exist without a physical symbol is difficult to grasp. Perhaps it is even more difficult to understand that this lack of physical possessions was considered an asset. The essence of the society of scholars mentioned by Miss Kibre resided in the supreme governing body of students, the Congregation. As long as this Congregation was not bound by immobile property, it was independent of local control. Its potential mobility gave the *studium* political and economic leverage, for when, as frequently happened, trouble arose between town and gown, part or all of the Congregation could threaten to or actually leave town until the loss of revenue and prestige forced the *borghesi* to come to terms. The architectural crystalization of the universities in the late fifteenth and subsequent century represented, according to Rashdall, the gradual triumph of the civil authorities over the independence of the student government of the Italian university.[17]

In contrast to the modern university which, at least at the time of this writing, is still governed by the academics, and is organized into colleges or schools that group faculty according to subject or groups of related subjects, the Italian medieval *studium* was run by the students, and was a loose association of colleges—or nations—in which students for their mutual protection (they were rarely citizens of the town, and rarely protected by its laws) had grouped together more or less according to their national origins. In Bologna by the mid-thirteenth century there were two nations, the *universitas citramontanorum* and the *universitas ultramontanorum*, each with its own rector, which included all of the students of civil and canon law. But law, if the most important, was not the only subject taught in Bologna.[18] It had already a famous *studium* of the liberal arts by 1000, although it was not until after 1300 that the jurists and the city recognized the independence of a corporation of arts and medicine (the two were associated in Bologna). After 1300, then, Bologna was divided in two: civil and canon law with its two nations on the one hand, and the arts and medicine on the other. This division was reflected in the physical separation of the *studium* from the thirteenth to the sixteenth century, for the medieval university like its modern counterpart needed some kind of shelter, even if as Miss Kibre observed, the modern campus was unknown.

Francesco Cavazza made a special study of the locations used for instruction in the city from the end of the thirteenth to the end of the sixteenth century, and presented his findings on a map of the center of the city showing the very disorganized physical location of the university.[19] In the early days instruction was given in rooms hired from private citizens by the students. For ordinary lectures the rooms of an urban palace were certainly sufficient, but what about popular lecturers, examinations, and convocations? What spaces in the medieval urban center were large enough to hold great crowds of students?

About the end of the thirteenth century the distribution of the schools in Bologna began to polarize, with a clear division between the law faculty south of the Piazza Maggiore in the old quarter called Porta Procula, and the arts and medicine faculty west of the piazza in the quarter called Porta Nova. A glance at Cavazza's map (Fig. 15) shows that the law schools occupied a series of irregular *palazzi* spreading from the center southward along the present Via D'Azeglio and eastward along the present Via Farini (formerly Via delle Scuole and Via dei Libri) toward the monastery of S. Domenico (Cat. 2), while the arts and medicine faculty occupied for the most part quarters scattered along the present Via IV Novembre (formerly the Via Porta Nova) from the piazza west past the monastery of S. Salvatore (Cat. 8) toward that of S. Francesco (Cat. 3). The map also makes very apparent that the two mendicant churches of S. Domenico and S. Francesco, other than the cathedral to the north of the Piazza Maggiore, were the only sizable congregational spaces in the center of town (S. Petronio on the piazza was begun only in 1390, and not actually constructed until after the middle of the fifteenth century). Until the building of the Archiginnasio in the late sixteenth century these churches, and their monasteries, were the physical focal points of the university. Examinations were held in the cathedral, while convocations, assemblies for the election of rectors, extraordinary lectures, and so forth were held in S. Domenico and S. Francesco, the churches of the friars. By 1301 the use of S. Domenico (Fig. 16) had become customary for both the *citramontani* and the *oltramontani* who constituted the law school. By 1340 it is clear that S. Francesco was being put to similar use by the doctors and artists, and in 1405 the statutes of this faculty specifically name this church as its place of assembly. In the late Middle Ages the modern dilemma of how the church might best serve the secular needs of the community had not yet arisen.

Such an administrative and physical division of the *studium,* with its focal points in the major monastic churches, was not peculiar to Bologna. In Ferrara,[20] for example, the artists convened in S. Domenico (Cat. 17) and the jurists in S. Francesco. Since Bologna was the most influential university in Italy, we can probably assume that the arrangement there was adopted elsewhere. The monasteries filled an architectural vacuum in the late medieval Italian university.

The universities north of the Alps, Paris for example, were primarily schools of theology in which the teaching was done by two distinct groups: the regular clergy (that is, the friars and monks) and the secular clergy (that is, those clerics outside of the orders and subject to the local bishop).[21] This led not only to the famous battles between these groups for control of the universities,[22] but to the division of the universities into two distinct foci: the monasteries on the one hand, and the colleges, such as the Sorbonne in Paris, on the other. Both needed libraries. In Italy, however, the university taught law primarily, and theological studies were at first left to the friars within their own monastic schools. The establishment by Urban V in 1364 of a school of theology as an integral part of the *studium* in Bologna meant in effect merely that the monastic schools opened their doors to students who were not monks; the friars still taught the subject.[23] In Italy, then, there was no rivalry, politically or architecturally, between the monasteries and the colleges, because there were almost no colleges (the Spanish College in Bologna being an exception). In Italy, the monasteries formed the unchallenged intellectual as well as physical focal points of the universities.

Guido Zaccagnini, in the only detailed study I have seen of a monastic school in an Italian university center, expressed the belief that S. Domenico in Bologna "became a kind of focal point for the university, the heart of which pulsated the entire intellectual life of the scholarly community." [24] This might be a slight exaggeration, but it is true that within the medieval Italian university town, books, as a part of the intellectual life, could be found in numbers in very few places: in the private libraries of wealthy collectors (and hardly accessible to any but friends of the owners), the collection of the cathedral,[25] or the monasteries. The exceptional Spanish College in Bologna received just 36 volumes at its foundation, and as late as 1453 possessed only just over one hundred.[26] The holdings of the Bolognese monasteries were much greater. Just before 1381 S. Domenico alone possessed about 630 volumes, including works on law, rhetoric, history, science, and mathematics (Cat. 2). An inventory dated 1421 of the books at S. Francesco in the same city lists 649 items (Cat. 3). The range of subjects included in these collections went beyond the obvious needs of the theologians resident within the monastery. Without doubt these libraries were "public," but the modern use of that term is so misleading that it is necessary to emphasize its limited meaning here. Those within the scholarly community who could qualify to use a monastic reference library in the late Middle Ages represented an exclusive group of students, professors, and clerics, and that exclusiveness was made visibly obvious by the monastery walls.[27]

With a little imagination then, and without contradicting the spirit of Miss Kibre's statement, we can say that the evidence outlined here suggests that in Italy from the late thirteenth through the late sixteenth centuries, the urban monasteries formed the "campus" of the urban university. The two most important parts of this "campus" were the church and the library. The library represents an area of overlap between two educational systems: monastery and university. As the depository of knowledge for both, the monastic reference library after 1300 in Italy grew to significant proportions, both as a collection of books and as a physical environment, as we shall see later on. But first we must ask why the monastery retained its role as the hub of the intellectual life of the Italian city even into the Age of Humanism.

OBSERVANTISM

Students of cultural history have made a neat distinction between the libraries of the Middle Ages and those of the Renaissance. The medieval library, they say, was typically a university or monastic collection, whereas that of the Renaissance was more often the private property of either a scholar or a prince.[28] As with all such generalizations there is some truth to this one, yet the mere fact of its currency obscures some rather important aspects of library history in the Renaissance. Because of the acknowledged decline of monastic life in the late fourteenth century, and the Burckhardtian emphasis upon the individual in the fifteenth, scholars such as Dorothy Robathan have been led to assert that by the middle of the fifteenth century, "the development of monastic libraries came to a halt," and more, that a survey of their collections after that date would be a "wasted effort." [29] Such state-ments stand in sharp contrast to the results of this study, which suggest a real flow-ering of monastic libraries and library architecture in the late fifteenth and early sixteenth centuries. How are we to account for such a flowering in the face of an arrested development in book collecting? The answer is, of course, that the monks did not stop acquiring books in the mid-fifteenth century. The old view that saw a sharp break between Middle Ages and Renaissance has gradually been discarded in favor of a view that recognizes a continuity between the two, even in Italy. This study reinforces the opinion that the culture of the quattrocento combines survival with revival, and that both must be included in any meaningful discussion of the period.

The Avignonese papacy from 1305 and the schism in the Western Church after 1378 did as much to rob monasticism of its moral and spiritual strength as the Black Death of the late 1340s had done to depopulate it. The institutionalized Church, and with it the religious orders, were attacked from within and without. From within came calls for reform; from without criticism and a decline in support. It is true that the religious fervor of these dark times sometimes took the form of large donations to religious institutions. S. Maria Novella in Florence, where the Spanish Chapel was built and decorated after 1350, was enriched through large donations in the second half of the fourteenth century.[30] But the histories of many other monastic houses dur-ing this period were very different, involving bankruptcy, depopulation, moral and spiritual lassitude, with the buildings in ruins or turned over to secular uses. The institution of the commenda, imposed upon many of these houses, usually created an administration the sole aim of which was to enrich itself from the monastic benefices. The Benedictine monastery of S. Giustina in Padua may be taken as an example. According to Ildefonso Tassi, S. Giustina was run by the ruling Carrara family until 1405 (when it fell to the Venetian Republic), and had degenerated into a "palace full of little princes" who used its "monies and benefices . . . to satisfy their desires."[31] In 1409 the religious community numbered three monks. Monastic collections also diminished, and as was typical, in 1422 the Dominicans in Perugia were forced to sell a missal to pay the butcher.[32] These appalling conditions seem to justify statements such as that of Miss Robathan cited above, but just at this nadir of Italian monastic history began one of those waves of monastic reform that peri-odically swept the pre-Lutheran Church.

What began as a heretical, underground reform movement within the Franciscan Order in the late fourteenth century came to be accepted by the Church as Observant-ism in the early fifteenth. It was recognized by the Council of Constance and given definitive form by Pope Eugene IV (1431-1447), and it became a dominant force within monasticism for the next century. If, despite the popularity of such Observantist preachers as St. Bernardine of Siena (1380-1444), the spiritual effect of the movement can be questioned, its architectural results seem beyond dispute. Its renewal of monastic vigor led to a renewal of confidence in reformed monasteries, and that in turn led to a renewal of private and religious support for the erection, rebuilding, and outfitting of monastic complexes. Outstanding evidence of this is the fact, reported by John Moorman, that 25 new Franciscan houses were established in Europe in the single year 1474.[33] All but one were for reformed or Observantist friars, and most were built at the expense of laymen.

Observantism was accepted by many of the Orders, large and small, new and old. Its general aim was to revitalize spiritually relaxed monastic houses by rededicating the monks or friars to the strict observance of the aims of an order as set forth in its original rule. If I concentrate upon the history of Observantism within the three most important Orders—the Franciscans, the Dominicans, and the Benedictines—it is only for the sake of brevity, and it should be borne in mind that in general the same story might be told of the lesser Orders as well—the Carmelites, the Servites, and the Regular Canons of the Lateran.

Observantist reform first sprang up within the Franciscan Order among those who objected to the relaxation of the Rule which had occurred immediately after Francis's death.[34] Under the guidance of his successor, Elias, and then St. Bonaventure, the Order became too worldly and educated for the "hard core" of Francis's followers. Great houses sprang up, following the lead of Elias's monument to the Founder at Assisi, but the Spiritualists rejected this negation of Francis's wishes and remained in absolute poverty and ignorance. They were soon labelled as heretics and were forced to take their protest underground. Recognition of this current within the Order was gained finally by Paoluccio Trinci da Foglino, who in 1368 was permitted to found a monastery based upon the strict observation of Francis's intentions. By his death in 1390 some 25 houses had joined him.

As I have said, the Franciscan Observants gained official stature from a decree of the Council of Constance, on September 27, 1415, recognizing the movement begun by Paoluccio. Although it mentioned only Franciscan Observants, this decree has been called the *magna charta* of the Observantist movement in general. Two years later St. Bernardine moved from the small monastery he had founded near Siena (later called the Osservanza) to the Franciscan Observantist house in Fiesole, and the long direction of the movement by the saint and his followers began. Despite the origins of the movement with the unlearned and penniless Spiritualists, St.

Bernardine, backed by Eugene IV, insisted upon establishing libraries and schools within Observantist houses, just as had existed almost from the beginning in the Conventualist, or unreformed, houses of the Order.

An Observantist movement also was begun within the Dominican Order under the guidance of the disciples of St. Catherine of Siena, especially Raimondo da Capua and Giovanni Dominici.[35] The latter was elected vicar general of S. Domenico in Venice in 1390, and this became the first Dominican Observantist house in Italy. The movement soon spread to other Dominican houses at Chioggia, Città di Castello, Cortona, Fiesole, Lucca, Fabriano, and Foligno, and with the election of Bartolomeo Texier as Master General of the Order (1426-1449), the success of Dominican Observantism was assured.

Perhaps the most successful of the Observantist movements in Italy was that within the Benedictine Order under the direction of Ludovico Barbo at S. Giustina in Padua (Cat. 43).[36] Barbo had been serving as the prior of the Observantist house of S. Giorgio in Alga in Venice (a center for reformist-minded monks around 1400 in which Gabriele Condulmer, later Eugene IV, was an active member) when he accepted the post of abbot of S. Giustina in 1409. He found three monks and a ruined monastery. His first task was to repopulate the house, make it economically viable, and then begin to rebuild. He called in a few Venetian associates; began a novitiate (1410); and started drawing recruits from the local university. By 1418 he had some 200 disciples. His great success led to housing problems, and he began to seek other monasteries, at first the vacant one of S. Fortunato at Bassano in 1411. This led to the formation, recognized by the Bull of Martin V on January 1, 1419 of a congregation of reformed houses named after the mother house at S. Giustina.

This original constitution of 1419 banded together four Benedictine houses: S. Giustina in Padua, the Badia in Florence, S. Giorgio Maggiore in Venice, and SS. Felice e Fortunato di Aimone in the diocese of Torcello. The constitution was badly conceived, however, and this first federation soon broke apart. The Florentine house under abbot Gomes Ferreira da Silva left the Congregation in 1428; it rejoined in 1441 after Gomes's departure (Cat. 20). The Venetian house separated itself from the union in 1430 when it was given in commenda to Condulmer (elected pope the following year), who returned it to the federation in 1443 (Cat. 52). After this early "crisis" the Congregation of S. Giustina regained its impetus when Eugene IV gave it a new constitution in 1432. It eventually absorbed other, less-successful Observantist monasteries within the Benedictine Order, and finally led to the union of most of the large Benedictine houses in Italy.[37]

We have seen that from the late thirteenth century on the monasteries were the foci of the intellectual life of the Italian city. In part because of their inherited intellectual resources in the form of large communal reference libraries, and in part because of the revitalization of monastic life through Observantism, the monasteries retained their importance throughout the quattrocento. Patronage of monasteries by laymen did not cease in the Renaissance despite the attacks by some humanists upon the corruption of the Orders. It is worth recalling that three of Brunelleschi's four major ecclesiastical commissions (Sto. Spirito, the Pazzi Chapel, and the rotunda at S. Maria degli Angeli) were part of rebuilding programs for monastic establishments. The fourth, S. Lorenzo, was for a canonry. Sto. Spirito, an Austin Hermit monastery, had an important collection of books, including among other items Boccaccio's library (Cat. 27). Partly because of this it was at least from the end of the fourteenth century a meeting place for such humanists as Coluccio Salutati, Niccolò Niccoli, Poggio, Giovanni di Lorenzo, and Roberto Rossi, all of whom gathered there under the leadership of Luigi Marsili.[38] Cosimo de' Medici, Niccolò, Palla Strozzi, Filippi di Ser Ugolino, and others frequently met at the Olivetan S. Maria degli Angeli under Ambrogio Traversari.[39] Niccolò's will directed that his famous collection of manuscripts be given to this monastery, and only the fact that he died in debt prevented this from happening.[40] The books went instead to Cosimo's new library at S. Marco (Cat. 23). These few examples can serve to indicate that patronage, learning, and much artistic energy were focused upon the urban monasteries in the quattrocento. To overlook this fact is to misunderstand the Italian fifteenth century.

Many of the monastic book collections of Italy were housed anew in the fifteenth century. And few are those whose histories in the quattrocento do not record one or more gifts of books or money for building from religious or secular patrons or collectors, among them outspokenly anti-monastic humanists. Many of the gifts were made to reformed houses, but even those that refused reform or were in no need of it profited by the reflected vitality of the Observantist movement. Monastic collecting, like monastic building, did not end with the fourteenth century.

The direct relationship between Observantist reform, architectural renewal, and continued or revitalized book collecting in the fifteenth century in Italy can be illustrated by a number of specific examples. There is, for instance, the rebuilding of the friary of S. Marco in Florence (Cat. 23), the reason for which is clearly given by Vespasiano da Bisticci: [41]

When the Pope [Eugene IV] was in Florence [first stay, 1434-1436] . . . he diligently attended to the reform of the Church, and made the Orders do the same on their own terms, and as well as he was able, made Observantists of the [unreformed] Conventualists. . . . His Holiness reformed S. Marco in Florence . . . there being within [this friary] ten or twelve friars, Pope Eugene reformed it, and wanted Cosimo [de' Medici] to fix up the place for the Dominican Observantists. . . . Cosimo promised to spend 10,000 ducats on it, and [finally] went to 40,000.

Whatever else might be said about Cosimo's motivation as a patron of the arts—whether it was a thirst for personal glory, a guilt complex, or antiproletarianism [42]—Vespasiano makes clear Cosimo's willingness to back financially the pope's desire for reform. Cosimo's faith in Observatism was such that he could pay for the rebuilding of this monastery after 1438, and place within it the large and very important library of humanistic manuscripts collected by Niccolò Niccoli. (We shall discuss the building erected to house that collection later.)

I pointed out above that S. Giorgio Maggiore in Venice and the Badia in Florence were two of the first four members of the Congregation of S. Giustina. S. Giorgio was given a library building designed by Michelozzo, if Vasari is correct, during Cosimo's exile to the Veneto in 1433 (Cat. 52). The fact that this was designed during the brief period of time when the monastery was again separated from the Congregation does not weaken the connection, for Eugene IV held it in commenda. The case of the Florentine Badia is even more illuminating (Cat. 20). Joined to the Congregation in 1415, the Badia broke away from 1428 to 1441. The library there was founded with a donation in 1421 by the humanist Antonio Corbinelli of his unparelleled collection of nearly 280 Greek and Latin manuscripts. Although some building activity went on in the monastery in the 1430s, the Badia apparently did not receive a room specifically designed to house this collection until the early sixteenth century. Such facts demonstrate the belief of both patron and humanist in the efficacy of Observantist reform.

One last example should put the point beyond controversy. In 1423 S. Giovanni di Verdara in Padua was occupied by one monk (Cat. 42). In 1430 it became affiliated with the Regular Canons of the Lateran, a minor reform movement founded in 1402. By 1446 the community had increased to 27 monks, who began to construct new buildings. In 1443 books were donated "pro utilitate studentium"; this was the first of a long series of donations that reflect a close bond between the monastery and the local university. Three donations of books are notable. In 1455 Battista del Legname, Bishop of Concordia, left the monastery 101 volumes. In 1478 Pietro da Montagnana, rector of the parish church of S. Fermo in Padua, left over ninety works. But both those splendid gifts were overshadowed by a third, a bequest in 1468 of 521 manuscripts by Giovanni Marcanova, a professor of medicine at the University of Padua.[43]

It was certainly in order to house a collection of books suddenly grown large that the existing library was erected in the late fifteenth century.

These examples, and others could be added, demonstrate that monastic collecting in Italy did not come to a halt in the middle of the fifteenth century. The reform movement known as Observantism was effective enough to inspire continued confidence in would-be patrons. The library buildings discussed in this essay and listed in the following catalogue, the monasteries that house them, and the many more Italian monasteries that were built or rebuilt in the fifteenth century that are yet unstudied, also prove the continuing vitality of this medieval institution in the quattrocento. In Renaissance Italy the urban monastery maintained its position as the focal point of intellectual life and artistic activity without interruption from the Middle Ages.

THE BUILDING PROGRAM

The program for the design of any building is the written or oral statement of the client to his architect or builder in which is set forth the requirements—symbolic as well as physical—that the building is meant to fulfill. That is, it must define the nature of the institution to be housed and the image that institution wishes to project, and, more specifically, list the spatial, structural, mechanical, and other factors that must form the basis for the architectural design. The formalization of such a program is, of course, of recent origin. There are no written building programs for the medieval or Renaissance monastic library, yet the library was built to satisfy certain specific needs, and these needs must once have been clear to builder and patron alike. Since they were embodied in the buildings, they can be read from the buildings, and checked against what documentary information we possess, especially inventories of monastic collections of the fourteenth and fifteenth centuries. Only when we have reformulated the building program of the medieval monastic library will we be ready to understand it as a work of spatial and structural art.

The monastic library of the Renaissance fulfilled requirements identical to those of the late medieval monastic library. To understand the one we must understand the other.

However, there are no recognized and unaltered fourteenth-century monastic libraries in Italy,[44] so we must rely on surviving inventories of the collections that existed in the fourteenth century to gain a general picture of the buildings erected to house them. We must first realize that the communal reference collection which interests us here was not always the only store of books in a monastery, for beside the church books in the sacristy there was often another collection under the abbot's thumb from which books were loaned to monks for private study. Although this lending library was at times larger than the reference collection, we know little about it, for most inventories give detailed information for the reference collection only. This fact, however, permits us to assume that it alone was given architectural consideration.

The earliest Italian inventory that has come to my attention and which reflects the presence of a reference and a lending collection is that of the library at the Cistercian abbey of S. Martino sul Monte Cimino near Viterbo.[45] It is dated 1305. Over 163 items are listed, of which 128 were in one room and divided by subject into 17 *scompartimenti*, 35 volumes were kept in the abbot's room, and the rest were scattered around the refectory (for reading during meals) and church. Another inventory of 1355, of the collection at S. Francesco in Pisa, numbers 377 works, of which 86 were chained to five desks.[46] But the inventories from which we can draw some specific conclusions about the fourteenth-century monastic library are those of S. Domenico in Bologna (before 1381; Cat. 2), S. Francesco in Assisi (1381; Cat. 1), S. Maria del Carmine in Florence (1391; Cat. 24), S. Antonio, the Franciscan house in Padua (1396; Cat. 40), and S. Marcello, the Servite house in Rome (1406; Cat. 50). The library of the Dominicans in Bologna, as we have seen, numbered some 630 volumes, of which 472 are listed separately as a chained reference collection, 145 are located in the sacristy, and 12 in the refectory. Assisi possessed nearly 700 volumes in two collections. The *libreria publica*, or communal collection, housed 181 books chained to reading desks, and the rest were kept in the *libreria secreta*, or storehouse. The Carmelites in Florence could boast of one of the largest book collections in fourteenth-century Italy. They had over 800 volumes, of which 113 are specifically listed in the library, 47 are noted as church books (and at least two of these were chained in the sacristy), 37 were in the hands of monks, and the bulk of the collection, 618 books, was "extra librariam," in the prior's quarters. The libraries at S. Antonio and S. Marcello were smaller, but their inventories reflect the same kind of distribution. The former housed 426 works, of which 114 were chained in the "armarium," and the latter had 67 items on reading desks in one room.

These five libraries, all but one in a university center, one Dominican, two Franciscan, one Carmelite, and one Servite, show to what extent Humbertus de Romanus's advice on the founding of reference libraries was followed in the fourteenth century, for all possessed one major library in which certain works were secured for communal use.

From the inventories just discussed we can guess how these libraries were furnished.

All mention reading desks. The manuscripts, often bulky, always precious, were stored and read in the same place: on a piece of wooden furniture called a *banco* in Italian or a *scamnum* in Latin (Figs. 11, 12, 24, 27, 36, 37). This is a combination seat and desk, with the books stored on the shelf below a sloping surface for the convenience of the reader. His comfort was also considered, for the wooden surfaces helped to insulate him from the cold and damp masonry room. The manuscripts were usually chained in place for security, in part because, as we have seen, they were not used solely by the inmates of the monastic establishment. Since each of these desks held on the average about a dozen volumes, it is obvious that a number of such desks was necessary to contain collections of more than a mere handful of books. The inventory of the reference library at S. Domenico in Bologna shows that the manuscripts were kept on 52 desks divided into two rows of 26 each. At Assisi they were chained to 18 desks also divided into two equal rows. At the Carmine in Florence only 14 desks, probably also divided into two equal rows although possibly in one long row, were needed. The library at S. Antonio in Padua was arranged in two rows of 12 reading desks each.

These inventories, then, provide us with a general picture of the requirements of the late medieval monastic reference library. What was needed was suitable housing for long rows of bulky reading desks divided by a central passage (and perhaps narrow side passages). It is obvious that these desks required adequate natural illumination, and this immediately suggests a rectangular room with the desks placed perpendicularly to the long walls with a regular series of windows for illumination.[47]

These requirements remained unchanged from the late thirteenth into the sixteenth century. The inventories of such fifteenth- and sixteenth-century libraries as those at S. Croce in Florence (Cat. 21), which in the fifteenth century contained two rows of 35 reading desks each, at the Badia in Florence (Cat. 20), which in the early sixteenth century had two rows of 15 reading desks each, at S. Domenico in Bologna (Cat. 2), which in the sixteenth century had two rows of 33 desks each, and of S. Francesco in Rimini (Cat. 48), which in the sixteenth century had 40 desks divided into two equal rows, to name just four, demonstrate that the requirements to house a library remained the same from one century to the next. The evidence we can gain from inventories is confirmed by the preserved books and desks at the Malatestiana (Cat. 11; Figs. 24, 27) and the Laurenziana (Cat. 22; Figs. 36-37). Despite this general continuity, however, it seems that the monastic library in late medieval Italy did not receive its definitive spatial form until the quattrocento.

We can only guess at the appearance of the fourteenth-century library. We do know, however, that the present library at S. Domenico in Bologna (Cat. 2) replaced an earlier reference room which was an unarticulated hall with exposed trusses over-head. The libraries at S. Croce in Florence, erected after 1427 perhaps from a project by Michelozzo (Cat. 21), and SS. Annunziata in Florence (Cat. 19), built certainly from Michelozzo's designs in the 1450s but perhaps designed as early as the 1430s, appear to have been of this same type. Neither is preserved unaltered, but the Annunziata library at least can be reconstructed in some detail from documents that can be checked against the existing structure. It too was a high unarticulated, or open, hall. It must have been a barn-like space with exposed decorated trusses above a two-story room lighted through regular series of late Gothic *bifore* in the long walls. There were originally two rows of desks divided by a central passage. Examination of the existing library wing at S. Croce convinced me that this too was a hall with exposed trusses. Since it was probably designed by the same architect at approximately the same time, this should come as no surprise.

The *bifore* of the library of the Annunziata can be seen now (Fig. 31), as in Ridolfo Ghirlandaio's view of the convent as it was in 1514, above shops to the left of the portico in front of the church (Fig. 30). The elevated position of these windows indicates that the library was on the upper floor of the monastery conveniently close to the dormitory. The library at S. Croce too was on the second story of the spinal building between the present first and second cloisters (Figs. 32-33). The elevated position of these two libraries was no accident. In fact, every other Italian medieval or Renaissance monastic library known to me is or was similarly elevated. There are no exceptions. A photograph of the second cloister at S. Croce taken on the morning of November 4, 1966 brings home clearly and forcefully the reason why all of these libraries were elevated (Fig. 34), and not incidentally illuminates another requirement of the building program for any library, medieval or modern. The flood of 1966 was not unique in Florentine history. The city has been periodically inundated by the Arno. Present-day Florentines seem to have learned little from their ancestors, however, for they stored books, manuscripts, and documents on the ground floor of the Archivio di Stato and the Biblioteca Nazionale, while the photograph taken on the morning of the flood of 1966 shows the fifteenth-century library of S. Croce high and dry even during the worst of that disaster. And what was and is true of Florence on the Arno was and is true of Piacenza on the Po, of Parma on the Parma, and many other towns. Even where there is no danger of flooding, as in Perugia or Monte-oliveto Maggiore near Siena, the ground floor of most buildings is too damp for the permanent storage of anything as valuable and perishable as manuscripts. Until our own day at least, books were never placed below the second floor for any length of time.[48] The added requirement of the building program, that the library be as dampproof as possible, dictated the elevated location of all monastic manuscript libraries in Italy.

To the requirements that libraries be large enough to accommodate rows of bulky desks, that natural illumination be adequate,[49] and that the manuscripts be kept as dry as possible, must be added one more: that the room be as fireproof as possible.[50] This final provision was not satisfied by the fourteenth-century builders, judging by the later rooms at S. Croce and SS. Annunziata in Florence. They were built with exposed wooden trusses that made them and their contents highly vulnerable to destruction by fire. That perhaps is one reason why none seems to have survived. The solution to this final requirement in the building program was given by Michelozzo when he designed the library for S. Marco in Florence (Cat. 23), probably after his earlier experiments with traditional library rooms at S. Croce (Cat. 21) and SS. Annunziata (Cat. 19) in Florence, and S. Giorgio Maggiore (Cat. 52) in Venice. With this step Michelozzo produced the definitive spatial form of the quattrocento monastic library, and thereby opened a new chapter in the history of library architecture.

BASILICA AND HALL

Preserved fifteenth- and sixteenth-century monastic libraries in Italy fall into two distinct spatial types: the basilica and the hall. The basilica, as its name implies, is a vaulted space divided into three aisles by two rows of columns (Fig. 24). The hall is an undivided room covered with either exposed trusses, a flat or coved ceiling (Figs. 22, 37), or one vault (Fig. 50). The basilica dominates monastic library design in the second half of the fifteenth century, but after 1500 as we shall see, the gradually changing needs of the library due to the invention of printing increasingly demanded the use of the hall. By the seventeenth century the basilica plan had disappeared.

The early history of the library in the Dominican friary of S. Marco in Florence is still somewhat obscure. The rebuilding of the friary began in 1438, and the library was finished by 1443, but it had to be rebuilt after an earthquake in the 1450s. Vasari says that Michelozzo originally designed it, and in the absence of other evidence, it is assumed here that this unchallenged attribution is sound, and that the library was rebuilt as originally built (Cat. 23; Figs. 38-42). The library occupies the upper floor of a wing extending northward from the dormitories surrounding the cloister of S. Antonino. It is a long narrow room divided into three aisles by two rows of Ionic columns supporting overhead vaults. The central passage is covered with a continuous barrel vault that is narrower than the cross vaults covering the side aisles. Architectural details are carved in *pietra serena,* and contrast with the stucco walls and vaults. The room was evenly lighted by a row of identical windows, one in each bay, in each side wall.

The location of this library within the monastery is not typical. Most of these libraries are located conveniently close to the dormitory as is that at S. Marco, but the library of S. Marco is located to one side of the cloister of S. Domenico and is perpendicular to the cloister of S. Antonino (Figs. 40-41).[51] The monastic library, which is rarely given any exterior architectural treatment to mark it apart from the other convent buildings, was most frequently located in the spinal building dividing major cloisters, either parallel or perpendicular to the church [52] (Figs. 13, 16, 32). Position was sometimes determined by pre-existent conditions, and often with regard to the requirements of the complex as a whole (Cat. 22). This was probably true at S. Marco.

Michelozzo's library is atypical in another respect. The present color scheme of gray-green *pietra serena* details and white stucco walls is more characteristic of traditional Florentine architecture than of the monastic libraries built in Renaissance Italy. The Malatestiana is more typical, in that green alone was used to cover its walls and vaults. This was done as well in the library of S. Domenico in Bologna (Cat. 2), and was seen by Serafino Razzi at S. Giovanni in Canale in Piacenza (Cat. 46) and at S. Andrea in Faenza (Cat. 16). It must have been the common color if the interiors were not frescoed, and probably was used on the basis of a recommendation by Isidore of Seville. This seventh-century bishop, in a passage on the decoration of libraries, recommended the use of green rather than gold, which is "hurtful to the eyes." [53]

The use of green in the interiors of these libraries and limited illumination from many small windows resulted in rooms which seem surprisingly dark to us. However, our preferences do not apply to the Renaissance. Justius Lipsius, the sixteenth-century humanist, who certainly spent much time in twilight spaces, says specifically that "a brilliant light is disturbing to the attention and makes writing difficult." [54]

The library at S. Marco is atypical in its placement and in its color scheme, if not in the quantity and quality of its interior illumination, but there is one more important characteristic of its design that became standard for monastic libraries for the next half-century at least. Filarete, in his description of the buildings erected by Cosimo de' Medici, singled out the vaulting in this basilical room as its unique feature, and Vasari echoed Filarete when he wrote that the library was "vaulted above and below." What Vasari meant was that the library was not only vaulted overhead, but also sustained from below by the vaults above the ground floor rooms (Fig. 41). By the use of masonry walls, floor, and vaults between the interior and the roof, Michelozzo created a fireproof room for the storage of manuscripts, and this solution to the ever-present danger of destruction by fire would alone single out this room as a major step in the evolution of library design.

Michelozzo revolutionized library architecture when he created a masonry container for the manuscripts at S. Marco by using the basilical spatial form, but the division of a room into three vaulted aisles is not his invention. Columnar spaces of two and three aisles are common in medieval monastic layouts, especially those of the Cistercians as demonstrated by Viollet-le-Duc's plan of the twelfth-century abbey at Clairvaux (Fig. 3). This system of continuous vaulting supported by rows of columns is a useful one for monastic establishments because of its flexibility: ranges of buildings could be erected from a uniform scheme, and then subdivided where necessary or desirable.[54a] Such spaces were probably once common in medieval France and Italy. A well-known French example is the thirteenth-century Knight's Hall at Mont St. Michel, but more important here is the fact that there are at least three such rooms from the thirteenth century that still exist in and around Florence. These are the so-called Pilgrim's Hall (Figs. 4-5) at the Cistercian Badia di S. Salvatore al Settimo,[55] down the Arno from the city; the lower dormitory (Figs. 6-7) on the north side of the Chiostro Grande of S. Maria Novella;[56] and another dormitory (Figs. 8-10; *not* originally the church) in the little-known monastery of S. Domenico al Maglio in the city.[57] All of these are vaulted spaces of three aisles divided by columns. Although none is the exact prototype of the library at S. Marco, any one of them, or a similar room, could have inspired its spatial form.[58]

These earlier vaulted rooms differ from the library at S. Marco in three significant ways. First, there is the simple and expected stylistic difference between a room of the thirteenth century and one of the fifteenth: the ribbed vaults of the earlier rooms produce a continuous linear articulation of the interior (Fig. 7) that gives way in the library at S. Marco to the effect of a smooth shell (Fig. 38). The second difference is more important. The vaults of the earlier rooms are all cross vaults, and all spring from the same level, but Michelozzo's library has a higher barrel vault above the central aisle. The earlier rooms have aisles of equal width, but Michelozzo adapted this existing spatial form to reflect the planning requirements of a monastic manuscript library. He made the central aisle narrower than those flanking it because it is merely a passageway between rows of reading desks occupying the side aisles, and different aisle widths suggested different vault forms. Michelozzo's choice of vault shapes was dictated by the way the room was to be used. The third and final difference between the earlier monastic spaces and Michelozzo's library at S. Marco is of extreme importance. All of the earlier Italian rooms stand on the ground (a fact that alone excludes them from consideration as libraries), but Michelozzo's library is raised to the upper level of the monastery, raised that is, above flood level.[59]

Michelozzo's concern to create a library that would be fireproof and dampproof caused certain difficulties of fabrication that he did not altogether solve. In fact, they were not to be solved until much later in the century. To recognize this we must look at the monastery of S. Marco as a whole. The rebuilding included a new church, the adjacent cloister of S. Antonino with its vaulted refectory below and dormitory above, vaulted ground-floor chapter house, small vaulted refectory for novices, and the library wing forming the east side of the cloister of S. Domenico. The church is not vaulted, but all other ground spaces are (Fig. 39). The dormitory and the library are the main areas of the second floor (Fig. 40). The dormitory (Fig. 43) is composed of a series of monks' cells set into a barnlike space covered with a gable roof sustained by exposed wood trusses. The cells are vaulted so that their diagonal thrusts counteract one another and there is no outward pressure on the upper exterior side walls. The library is very different (Fig. 38). There the greater desire for fireproof construction demanded an all-masonry envelope, the overhead vaults of which produce a lateral thrust outward against the exterior walls. This thrust is countered by iron tie-rods, of course, but the whole edifice in section looks precariously flimsy to me (Fig. 41), especially since the inner columns of the library are resting upon what looks like thin air (in reality they rest on the back of the shallow vault above the small refectory).

The awkwardness of this structural section, its discontinuity between one floor and the other (and Michelozzo built both), suggests that Michelozzo was not sure of himself in creating elevated vaulted spaces. This is rather surprising, not only because Michelozzo used vaults elsewhere (with such frequency that Heydenreich could characterize his *oeuvre* as a *Wölbestil*[60]), but more because of the fourteenth-century Florentine tradition of building masonry vaults on a grand scale that culminated in Brunelleschi's majestic cupola, in construction during these very years. I have found no satisfactory answer to this surprising dichotomy, although there does not seem to have been precedent for raising vaults to the second floor of a monastic building, and there was a general reluctance to create large elevated vaulted spaces during the mid-fifteenth century. This is apparent even in Brunelleschi's work after the cupola.[61]

The inexplicable awkwardness of the structural section of the library wing at S. Marco does not, however, reduce the quality of Michelozzo's achievement. His apt solution to the requirements of a dry, fireproof room for the storage and consultation of manuscripts is almost a textbook example of fine architecture as the manifestation of the building program. Rows of desks divided by a central passageway were contained within an elevated masonry shell, and even the shape of that shell conforms to the program. The central passageway is surmounted by a continuous barrel vault, whereas the side aisles containing the books and benches with their multiplicity of foci (at least one per book) are surmounted by series of cross vaults represented in plan by series of focal X's. So Michelozzo's library is a perfect demonstration of what we in this century have called "functional" architecture; of what, for example, Louis Sullivan meant when he advised architects to seek the solution to a problem within the statement of the problem. It is not surprising, then, that the library at S. Marco became the archetype of the monastic library in Renaissance Italy.

The basilical form created by Michelozzo for the Dominican library in Florence radiated outward from Tuscany to the whole of north and central Italy (Fig. 14). The earliest of the surviving basilical libraries, that by Matteo Nuti at Cesena (Cat. 11), can be linked to Florence through Nuti's work under Alberti at Rimini. Our next recorded example is the library at S. Domenico in Bologna (after 1461; Cat. 2), erected during the years when the Florentine follower of Michelozzo, Pagno di Lapo, was working at the church. The library of the Dominicans at S. Maria delle Grazie in Milan was also built in the 1460s (Cat. 36). It was built under the aegis of Gaspero Vimercato, and tradition records that he resorted to Cosimo de' Medici's advice. (There is also a tradition that Michelozzo himself was in Milan at this time, but if this is true his connection with this library can have been no more than tenuous.) The next preserved basilical library is that at S. Domenico in Perugia (1474; Cat. 45), erected under the direction of Leonardo Mansueti, Master General of his Order, who had held the chair of Logic at the *studium* in Florence while Michelozzo's library at S. Marco was in construction.

By the turn of the century the basilical form had become common for the library, and it was used throughout the cinquecento, but it was changed in some buildings after the first quarter of the century. The monastic library shown by Giorgio Vasari il Giovane in his *Città ideale* of 1598 (Cat. 28; Fig. 59) is a pastiche of ideas then a century and a half old; the library S. Agostino in Cremona, begun in 1589, seems to have been a rather curious attempt to squeeze an early Baroque room out of this late medieval spatial form (Cat. 14). The basilical form was superseded in the real Baroque monastic library by the hall, which began to reappear at the end of the quattrocento, as we shall see.

We can trace the architectural development of the basilical type during the years of its ascendency, an ascendency so complete in the second half of the fifteenth century in Italy that Antonello could use the basilical form in the background of his *St. Jerome in His Study* as a universal symbol of the monastic library (Frontispiece). The basic similarity of these rooms precludes the necessity to examine each in detail here. Rather we can consider the development of the type as a whole from four different points of view: structural system, vaulting, relationship of the library to the rest of the monastery, and spatial form. This discussion must obviously be limited to preserved or minutely recorded lost examples, so generalization must be based upon few data, and indeed, data that end early in the sixteenth century. But even if the conclusions in the main are founded upon evidence accidentally and insufficiently preserved, the discussion itself will reveal aspects of the development essential to an understanding of the monastic library in Italy.

The makeshift character of the two-story structural system of the library building at S. Marco in Florence (Fig. 41), with its disconnected upper and lower stories, is reflected in the three libraries built after S. Marco. That at Cesena rests upon a ground floor divided into just two aisles, so that upper and lower internal supports are not aligned (Fig. 25). The same lower structure is found again at S. Domenico in Bologna (Figs. 17-19), but here the upper library is shifted over so that its walls and columns are supported directly from below. A section through the library building at S. Maria delle Grazie in Milan (Fig. 44) was similar to that of S. Domenico in Bologna, but less sophisticated, for one row of library columns was not aligned with the row of columns on the floor beneath. Not until S. Domenico in Perugia (Cat. 45), apparently, and S. Sepolcro in Piacenza, certainly, do we find the ideal solution (Cat. 47; Fig. 56): a continuous, symmetrically balanced structural system in which the inner columns rest upon parallel walls of the floor below and the outer walls rest upon cloister arcades, in a neat alternation of solid and void. The same system is present at S. Giovanni Evangelista in Parma (Cat. 44), and the three-story system at S. Vittore in Milan (Cat. 37) is similar. The room at Monteoliveto Maggiore (Cat. 39), however, is out of step here (as we shall see that it is in nearly every other category), for none of its inner columns is directly supported from below. But even where we find the mature system, as at Piacenza, these lofty vaulted structures, with their nearly invisible tie rods and thin exterior walls set upon the arched voids of the cloister arcades, strike us as daring feats of vector equilibrium.

If the development of the structural system leads toward the integration of parts into a balanced unit, the various solutions to the problem of vaulting the basilica seem to describe an irregular course toward the same goal, toward spatial unity. We have seen that Michelozzo solved the problem of covering the narrower central aisle by using a barrel vault (Figs. 14A, 38), as did the architects of the libraries at Cesena (Figs. 14B, 24) and Bologna (Figs. 14C, 19). The architect of the library at S. Maria delle Grazie in Milan, however, switched to cross vaults, and this created a problem he could not completely solve (Figs. 14D, 45). The wider aisles were covered by only seven vaults each, whereas there were nine smaller ones above the narrower center. The discrepancy in the number of vaults above the center and above the sides was only partly obscured by building the central vaults higher. At Perugia (Figs. 14E, 53) the architect solved the problem inherent in the overall use of cross vaults by slightly altering the spatial form established by Michelozzo on the basis of the requirements of the building program. He made all three aisles equal, so that all of his vaults could be of the same size and shape. Although Alessio Tramello, the architect of S. Sepolcro in Piacenza (Figs. 14F, 55), also divided his library into equally wide aisles, he inexplicably chose different vault forms to cover the center and side aisles, and at S. Vittore in Milan (Figs. 14G, 48) the architect followed Tramello's vaulting scheme but made his central passage wider than his side aisles, thus flattening the arch of the central vaults. At Monteoliveto Maggiore (Figs. 14H, 49) the architect chose to follow the example of Michelozzo's co-Tuscan library at S. Marco. Finally at Parma, the architect created aisles of equal width (Figs. 14I, 51), and used identical cross vaults throughout the room. He also enhanced the unity inherent in the use of equal units by springing all of these vaults from points equidistant from the floor. So we now have come full circle. The library at Parma refers back to our starting point: to the late medieval vaulted rooms that formed the inspiration for Michelozzo's library at S. Marco. Like those earlier rooms at S. Maria Novella (Fig. 7) and S. Domenico al Maglio in Florence (Fig. 9), the library at Parma is a sum achieved by the addition of equal parts, but this integration was accomplished by compromising the appropriate spatial form established by Michelozzo.

The integration of parts through compromise also marks the development of the relationship between the basilical library and the rest of the monastery. For the purpose of brevity I will select three monasteries to illustrate this development.

The library in S. Marco in Florence (Fig 38) is the only vaulted room on the upper floor, for the dormitories are composed of low vaulted cells set into a larger space covered with trusses (Fig. 43). There is no internal continuity between the form and structure of the library and the form and structure of the rest of the monastery (Figs. 39-40). The two are disconnected, like the floors of the library itself (Fig. 41), and this cannot have been the result of piecemeal construction because the monastery rose in one campaign. Michelozzo satisfied the requirements of each part separately, without regard for the unity of the monastery as a whole. At S. Sepolcro in Piacenza, in contrast, both dormitory and library are vaulted throughout. The dormitory is composed of a high cross-vaulted corridor that is broader than the lower, vaulted, lateral spaces divided into monks' cells. As we know, the library is also composed of vaulted center and side aisles, but all three aisles are of equal width (Figs. 14F, 55). Although there is now a closer relationship between the two parts of the monastery, the library in Piacenza retains something of its own spatial character. In contrast, the whole monastery of S. Vittore al Corpo in Milan is composed of one spatial section throughout. The upper floor of the dormitory (Fig. 46) is very like that at Piacenza, with a high vaulted central corridor (the vaults lighted through circular windows in every other bay) flanked by narrower lateral areas that once were divided into cells. This same section carries through the spinal building separating cloisters, and so dictates the exceptional spatial form of the library located on the top floor of that building (Fig. 48). The architect of S. Vittore was able to develop a totally integrated monastery but, in doing so, he was forced to make the central passage of his library wider than the side aisles, and that contradicts its function as a mere passageway (Fig. 14G).

In the development of the structural system we found an inconsistent but recognizable tendency toward a balanced integration of parts. In the evolution of the vaulting we found a circular course of experiments leading back to the simple, integrated forms from which the development sprang. Continuity was the goal toward which the development of the library in relation to the whole complex led us. We shall find that the evolution of the spatial form of these rooms plots a meandering course toward these same objectives, that is, toward unity (Fig. 14). The mere recitation of the ratios of length to width in these libraries would be sufficient to suggest the direction of this development, but these changing proportions are closely linked to the vault formations and window openings. They are linked, that is, to those articulating elements that define and characterize an architectural space. We must consider all of these elements together if we are to gain an exact understanding of this development.

The earliest libraries, at S. Marco in Florence (Figs. 14A, 38) and S. Francesco in Cesena (Figs. 14B, 24), are long narrow spaces about four times as long as they are wide.[62] Their pronounced lengthiness is emphasized by the continuous barrel vault above the central passage in each (and this is even reinforced at S. Marco by the molding that outlines this vault), and by the many small, regularly spaced windows running down both side walls (and this is even reinforced at Cesena by the engaged half-columns and the doubling of the windows). The library at S. Domenico in Bologna (Figs. 14C, 19) is much broader, only about two and a half times as long as it is wide, but the barrel vault still was used, and there is still a multiplicity of windows to emphasize the length of the room. The next two libraries, at S. Maria delle Grazie in Milan (Fig. 14D) and S. Domenico in Perugia (Figs. 14E, 53), are slightly narrower again, about three times as long as they are wide, but the emphasis on the length has been reduced slightly because cross vaults were used instead of a barrel vault. The windows in Perugia were placed in every other bay, and this slows down their effect of receding when the room is viewed from the entrance. The library at S. Sepolcro in Piacenza (Figs. 14F, 55) is also just about three times as long as it is wide. Again there is a window in every bay. The cross-vaults above the central passage still tend to reinforce the direction of the room because they are placed higher than the lateral vaults in which there is also a continuous severy from end to end of the room. The trend toward broader spaces is resumed at S. Vittore al Corpo (Figs. 14G, 48) and at Monteoliveto (Figs. 14H, 49); both are about two and a half times as long as they are wide. The central vaults at Milan are still higher than their neighbors, however, and the barrel vault and its framing molding reappear at Monteoliveto. The windows in the latter are more what we would expect, for they were placed only in every other bay, although only on one side. Also, as in the library at Cesena, pilasters along the walls add to the feeling of length in the space given by the rows of free-standing columns. Finally, at S. Giovanni Evangelista in Parma (Figs. 14I, 51), the library has been broadened; it is just over one and a half times as long as it is wide. All the cross-vaults spring from the same height above identical rectangular bays, the long dimensions of which are perpendicular to that of the room. The longer walls have windows in every other bay, but the doors at either end of the room are flanked by blind windows, so that all four walls have nearly identical articulation.

It must be observed, too, that the reading desks in S. Giovanni Evangelista would have interlocked smoothly with the architecture of the room, whereas the tops of the reading desks in the Malatestiana in Cesena were placed awkwardly against the columns about half way up their shafts (Fig. 24). This jarring confrontation of architecture and furnishings was probably avoided at Parma (Fig. 51) and at S. Corona in Vicenza (Cat. 54; Fig. 60) by using pedestals to raise columns into full view above the desks. The integration of furnishings and architecture has been said to have been Michelangelo's contribution in the Laurenziana,[63] but these pedestals suggest that an attempt to integrate these two elements had already been made. Thus, only the slightly greater length of the room, the rows of columns, and the direction of the Ionic capitals recall at Parma the longitudinal effect of the earlier libraries, but everything else in the room works against that association.

There is nothing absolutely consistent about the development of these libraries, yet it does indicate a growing urge by the first quarter of the sixteenth century to create units of space of greater and greater coherence and harmony, and Michelozzo's spatial form was gradually sacrificed to meet this desire. We witness a tendency to form spaces that move ever closer to the openness and unity of the undivided hall.

We have seen that the fourteenth-century monastic library seems to have been built as an undivided hall, as are those altered rooms at S. Croce (Cat. 21) and SS. Annunziata in Florence (Cat. 19). Then Michelozzo designed the library at S. Marco, departing from that tradition and resorting to the basilical space with such success that this form dominated library architecture for more than a half-century. Halls begin to be built again at the end of the fifteenth century, however. The hall added to the basilical space at S. Domenico in Bologna in 1496 (Cat. 2), the hall erected about 1490 at S. Barnaba in Brescia (Cat. 9; Figs. 20, 22), and the vaulted hall built also about 1490 in the monastery of S. Giovanni di Verdara in Padua (Cat. 42; Fig. 50) are preserved examples of this revival. Whereas the basilica exactly suited the storage of manuscripts in rows of reading desks divided by a central passage, the reappearance of the hall can only be explained by the changes wrought in the building program by the advent of printing.

After the introduction of printing in Italy in 1465, more and more printed books were added to the monastic library inventories.[64] The greater economy effected by printing increased the number of books available and hence increased the size of collections.[65] The relative inexpensiveness and availability of books meant that it was no longer necessary to chain them to reading desks as precious objects.[66] And the large folio gradually gives way to the smaller quarto, octavo, and so on. For these reasons, the space-consuming rows of bulky reading desks sticking out from the wall into the room gradually were replaced by bookshelves set flat against the wall. The books could be stored upright on the shelves and read at tables or desks placed in the room. This had a direct impact upon the spatial form of the library, for the low vaulted basilica filled with columns was less well suited to tiers of flat bookcases than the hall with its high straight walls. The hall also became practical because books were easier to read, first because humanistic script was used, and then clear uniform type. The semilegibility of the older script had frequently made the reader voice what he read,[67] and the high-backed reading desks helped to isolate one mumbling medieval scholar from another (Fig. 11). This became less and less necessary as printing encouraged the spread of silent reading.

The sixteenth century saw the gradual replacement of the basilica by the hall. The origins of this shift can be found in the late fifteenth century, as the halls at S. Domenico in Bologna, at S. Barnaba in Brescia, and at S. Giovanni di Verdara in Padua indicate, and yet, the use of shelves rather than reading desks in the library at S. Agostino in Cremona was described in 1599 as a "new invention" (Cat. 14). There is no sharp break between the use of one spatial type and the use of the other, just as there is no sharp break between the production of manuscripts and the introduction of printed works.[68] Michelangelo's Laurentian Library in Florence is a hall with reading desks; the library at S. Agostino in Cremona was a (modified) basilica with shelves. Manuscripts and incunabula, basilicas and halls, overlapped for a century or more, but during the course of the sixteenth century it became increasingly clear to which the future belonged.

THE LAURENZIANA

The reading room of the Laurentian Library in Florence—and I am concerned exclusively with the reading room despite the fact that in recent art historical studies the *ricetto,* or entrance hall, has often assumed the identity of the whole library [69]— stands midway on the course of the changeover from basilica to hall. The definitive design was established by Michelangelo in 1524 (Cat. 22). It thus comes after the continuous development just discussed, and it would be surprising if the previous history of an identical building type did not have some bearing upon Michelangelo's design; nonetheless, most writers have chosen to ignore this development. Charles de Tolnay is one of the few serious scholars even to mention earlier libraries in connection with the Laurentian, but even he misunderstood them. "The Laurentian Library," he wrote in Italian in 1951, "is the architectural design in which Michelangelo expresses most clearly the originality of his conception. For the first time in the history of art the interior of a library was conceived not by the application of the laws of religious architecture, but according to an idea corresponding to its specific function." [70] I believe that with this enough has been said in previous pages to correct the misconception that the basilical library was never conceived as a church.[71]

If recent critics of the Laurentian Library have forgotten or misunderstood the development of the monastic library prior to Michelangelo, neither he nor his patron,

Pope Clement VII, a Medici, ignored it. Both certainly had the earlier Medici library at S. Marco in mind during the design of the Laurentian. Michelangelo's first design, for example, was for a library divided into Latin and Greek collections, like the earlier Medici library, and Clement specifically mentioned the desks at S. Marco as a standard for those at S. Lorenzo (Fig 36). The Laurentian is more traditional than novel in its cultural significance; in this respect there is little difference between Clement's library at S. Lorenzo and Cosimo's at S. Marco. The monasteries maintained their traditional position as foci of urban intellectual life into the Age of Humanism. That reputation had its origins in the Middle Ages; so, in this sense, Clement's library is thoroughly medieval.

Architecturally too the Laurentian retains the marks of tradition (Fig. 37). Ackerman's analysis of the room stressed the problem of construction encountered by Michelangelo.[72] The walls were to be placed upon walls already two stories high. This superimposed weight had to be kept to a minimum, and this meant that a masonry vault above the room was out of the question. So Michelangelo was forced to design an unvaulted hall, despite the fact that its wood ceiling would be less fire-resistant than the vaulted basilica. If these conditions forced the hall form upon Michelangelo, he nonetheless recalled the basilica in his design. He combined the two types of libraries in the interior of the reading room: the hall, as at S. Croce (Cat. 21) or SS. Annunziata (Cat. 19) and the basilica, as at S. Marco (Cat. 23) and elsewhere. Michelangelo must have recognized the expressive aptitude of the basilical form. Although the Laurentian is basically a hall, it is a long narrow space about four times as long as it is wide, with reading desks like earlier libraries (Fig. 35). The form of the basilica can be seen in the handling of the walls and ceiling (Fig. 37). The tripartite division of the end walls is carried the length of the room by corresponding divisions of the floor and ceiling, and by the central passage between reading desks. The rows of columns that appear to recede down the center of a divided library have been turned into rows of pilasters. Not even the integration of architecture and furniture is novel here, if I am correct in assuming that the pedestals at Parma (Fig. 51) and Vicenza (Fig. 60) raised the column bases above the desks in those earlier libraries. Just as in the *Creation of Eve* on the Sistine Ceiling Michelangelo made use of such a quattrocento prototype as Jacopo della Quercia's *Creation of Eve* on the Porta Magna of S. Petronio in Bologna, here he pays homage to the quattrocento basilical library, and no one who comes into the Laurentian reading room fresh from the library at S. Marco can miss this association (Figs. 37-38).

The Laurentian became a prime source of inspiration for the architects who built open monastic libraries during the Baroque period, the first of which was erected in the Escorial north of Madrid in the 1560s. But its true position within the development of monastic library architecture is best characterized as a brilliant reinterpretation, or better, recapitulation, of the tradition outlined here.

The characteristics of tradition retained in the Laurentian Library are indicative of the general conclusion that emerges from this study of the history of the monastic library in Italy. Monasticism, revived by the advent of the friars in the thirteenth century, and with the impetus of the Observantist movement of the fifteenth century, carried on its traditional role as the guardian of intellectual affairs even into the sixteenth century. Fifteenth-century monastic libraries were housed in rooms based on a medieval spatial form, revived by Michelozzo, that reflected the traditional needs of the manuscript collection. The basilical library ties the architecture of the fifteenth and sixteenth centuries to that of the thirteenth, just as Observantism ties fifteenth-century monasticism to its thirteenth-century, and earlier, origins. The break in this tradition of medieval monastic library architecture comes not in the fifteenth century but late in the sixteenth. Michelangelo's library at S. Lorenzo in Florence marks a turning point in the planning of monastic libraries while summarizing the last phase of medieval library architecture begun by Michelozzo at S. Marco.

Notes

1. V. da Bisticci, *Vite di uomini illustri del secolo XV*, eds. P. D'Ancona and E. Aeschlimann, Milan, 1951, p. 27: *"Usava dire che dua cose farebbe s'egli mai potesse ispendere, ch'era in libri, e in murare: e l'una e l'altra fece nel suo pontificato."*

2. But we cannot blame all destruction on Napoleon. Two fifteenth-centuries libraries (Cats. 36, 54) were destroyed as recently as World War II.

3. M. Battaglini, "La soppressione dei conventi nella repubblica romana giacobina," *Palatino*, IX, 1965, pp. 13-23. In Venice the suppressions of 1806-1810 accounted for the spoliation of at least 25 monastic libraries. Desks and shelves were sold for lumber, and the books carted away to public depositories. P. LaCute ("Le vicende delle biblioteche monastiche veneziane dopo la soppressione napoleonica," *Venezia, rivista mensile della città*, VII, 1929, p. 612) quotes the following rather melodramatic eye-witness account of the rape of the library at S. Giobbe:

   Noi li vedemmo spezzarsi e, sensa avvertenza alcuna, farsi in brani; nè abbiamo potuto a lungo fermarci presenti a tale distruzione, sia perchè l'animo nostro troppo soffriva, sia perchè al rompersi di quei legni, l'odore di quei vecchi cipressi era così forte da far dolere la testa.

   The similar fate of some monastic libraries in Abruzzi and Molise is discussed in A. Gallo, "Biblioteche abruzzesi e molisane," *Accademie e biblioteche d'Italia*, IV, 1930, pp. 126-143, and in the *Guida storica e bibliografica degli achivi e delle biblioteche d'Italia*, Rome, VI, 1932-1940, pt. 1.

4. London, National Gallery. Neither the date nor the attribution is documented, but most critics now give the work to Antonello. The setting has always puzzled commentators, who have usually called it a church (the best discussion is in R. Papini, "Interpretazione di Antonello," *La Rinascista*, III, 1940, pp. 493-494). The details of the architecture are admittedly a little fantastic; nonetheless, I think the painting gives a rather accurate depiction of the interior of a monastery with St. Jerome sitting at his desk, inexplicably in the center of a dormitory corridor. A monk's cell opens into the left background, and a basilical library recedes into the right background. No reading desks are shown in the library because they would have cluttered Antonello's painted space just as they did the real space of an actual library. The local realism of this painting extends to its architectural setting. See also M. Brawne, *Libraries*, New York, 1970, p. 9.

   A second painted representation of a monastic library space that has come to my attention is in the Museum of Fine Arts, Budapest. Sassetta's *St. Thomas Inspired By The Holy Ghost*, a predella panel from the altar painted between 1423 and 1426 for the Arte della Lana in Siena, shows the saint praying before an altar on the left, with courtyard in the middle background, and a library to the right (Fig. 12). It would seem to be a single, vaulted space with one row of reading desks, an entrance at the near end, and an oculus lighting the other end. See J. Pope-Hennessy, *Sassetta*, London, 1939, pp. 6 ff., and M. Boskovits, *Tuscan Painting Of The Early Renaissance*, New York, 1968, pls. 9-10.

5. Only two minor descriptive (rather than historical) publications have been devoted specifically to the architecture of the monastic library in Italy. Both are by Giovanni Cecchini: a booklet, issued

"fuori commercio," entitled *6 biblioteche monastiche rinascimentali*, Milan, 1960, and an article rather misleadingly called "Evoluzione architettonico-strutturale della biblioteca pubblica in Italia dal secolo XV al XVII," *Accademie e biblioteche d'Italia*, XXXV, 1967, pp. 27-47. There have been other brief, and frequently inaccurate discussions in larger works, such as J. W. Clark, *The Care of Books*, Cambridge, 2d ed., 1909, pp. 193 ff., or F. Cognasso, *L'Italia nel rinascimento*, Turin, I, 1965, pp. 438-455.

The contemporary libraries of some other European countries have received better treatment. For England, see B. H. Streeter, *The Chained Library*, London, 1931; for Germany, E. Lehmann, *Die Bibliotheksräume der deutschen Klöster im Mittelalter*, Berlin, 1957. Those in France await comprehensive study.

Other works on library architecture, some of which contain material on Italy, will be found in the bibliography.

6. G. Becker, *Catalogi bibliothecarum antiqui*, Bonn, 1885. Cf. T. Gottlieb, *Ueber mittelalterliche Bibliotheken*, Leipzig, 1890 (reissued Graz, 1955), pp. 179-254; and J. W. Thompson, *The Medieval Library*, Chicago, 1939 (reissued New York, 1965), p. 130.

7. This library is discussed by Lehmann, *Bibliotheksräume*, pp. 6, 43.

8. Clark, *Care of Books*, pp. 70 ff.. Cf. M. Aubert, *L'Architecture cistercienne en France*, Paris, 2d ed., II, 1947, pp. 39-47 for transalpine parallels.

9. H. J. Chaytor, *From Script to Print*, New York, 1967, p. 10. The early tenth-century Customs of Cluny cited by Clark (*Care of Books*, p. 57) mention the distribution of one book per year to each monk. If he had not read it through, he had to confess in Lenten Chapter "his want of diligence."

10. The eleventh-century rebuilding of Monte Cassino provided the library there with its own building, but this is a remarkable exception. See C. H. Haskins, *The Renaissance of the Twelfth Century*, Cambridge, 1927, p. 71, and Thompson, *Medieval Library*, p. 175.

11. K. W. Humphreys, *The Book Provisions of the Medieval Friars 1215-1400*, Amsterdam, 1964, p. 33:

> *Item ad ipsum pertinet providere quod in aliquo loco silentii et apto sit aliquis pulpitus magnus vel plures in quibus ligentur aliqui libri bene legibiles quibus frequentius fratres indigent cum habentur. . . .*

I follow Humphreys in much that I say about the reference library.

12. For monastic schools see H. Felder, *Geschichte der wissenschaftlichen Studien im Franziskanerorden bis um die Mitte des 13 Jahrhundert*, Freiburg im B., 1904 (French and Italian translations exist); Célestin Douais, *Essai sur l'organisation des études dans l'ordre des Frères Prêcheurs au treizième et au quatorzième siècle (1216-1342)*, Paris-Toulouse, 1884; H. M. Féret, "Vie intellectuelle et vie scolaire dans l'order des Frères Prêcheurs," *Archives d'histoire dominicaine*, I, 1946, pp. 1-37.

13. Cf. F. Ehrle, *I Più antichi statuti della facoltà teologica dell' università di Bologna*, Bologna, 1932, p. lxxii.

14. H. Rashdall, *The Universities of Europe in the Middle Ages*, eds. F. M. Powicke and A. B. Emden, London, 1936, and H. S. Denifle, *Die Entstehung der Universitäten des Mittelalters*, Berlin, 1885, are the standard works on the medieval university. N. Schachner, *The Mediaeval Universities*, New York, 1962, is a reliable and readable popular account.

15. Padua seems an exception. The university there received its first building from Francesco Carrara in 1399 (Rashdall, II, p. 20). Perugia received its building in 1512 (G. Ermini, *Storia della università di Perugia*, Bologna, 1947, pp. 376 ff.) Lorenzo il Magnifico provided Pisa with a home in 1492 (Rashdall, II, p. 62). Ferrara first received its own building in 1567 (A. Visconti, *La storia dell'università di Ferrara [1391-1950]*, Bologna, 1950, pp. 67 ff.). Late fifteenth-century projects for university buildings are preserved for Siena (*Il taccuino senese di Giuliano da San Gallo*, ed. R. Falb, Siena, 1902, pls. XXI, XXIX) and Rome (J. Wasserman, "Giacomo della Porta's Church for the Sapienza in Rome and Other Matters Relating to the Palace," *Art Bulletin*, XLVI, December, 1964, p. 501).

16. P. Kibre, *The Nations in the Mediaeval Universities*, Cambridge, Mass., 1948, p. ix.

17. Rashdall, I, pp. 187-188; II, pp. 61-62.

18. *Ibid.*, I, p. 87 ff.

19. F. Cavazza, *Le scuole dell'antico studio bolognese*, Milan, 1896. See also A. M. Matteucci, "Conventi e collegi: lo Studio in tutta la città," *Bologna. Centro storico*, Bologna, 1970, pp. 229-242 (Catalogue of an exhibition held in the Palazzo d'Accursio, 1970).

20. Visconti, *Storia dell'università di Ferrara*, p. 19.

21. Rashdall, I, pp. 89 ff., 250 ff.
22. Schachner, *Mediaeval Universities*, pp. 84 ff.
23. G. Zaccagnini, *Storia dello studio di Bologna durante il rinascimento*, Geneva, 1930, pp. 35 ff.
24. G. Zaccagnini, "Le scuole e la libreria del convento di S. Domenico in Bologna," *Atti e memorie della R. Deputazione di storia patria per la provincia di Romagna*, Ser. IV, XVII, 1927, pp. 228-327.
25. A. Sorbelli, *La biblioteca capitolare della cattedrale di Bologna nel secolo XV*, Bologna, 1904. An inventory of this collection dated 1451 (pp. 83 ff.) lists 329 volumes, some of which contain more than one work.
26. The original donation is listed in Berthe M. Marti, *The Spanish College at Bologna in the Fourteenth Century*, Philadelphia, 1966, pp. 77-82. For the fifteenth-century inventory see C. Piana, *Ricerche su le università di Bologna e di Parma nel secolo XV*, Quaracchi, 1963, pp. 53-55. This inventory mentions 16 desks with roughly seven volumes per desk. See also M.-H. Laurent, *Fabio Vigili et les bibliothèques de Bologne*, Vatican City, 1943, pp. xxv-xxvi, 1-10, 175-179.

   Contrast these small figures to those recorded for the Sorbonne in Paris: 1017 volumes in 1290, and 1722 by 1338. See B. L. Ullman, "The Sorbonne Library and the Italian Renaissance," in his *Studies in the Italian Renaissance*, Rome, 1955, pp. 41-53, and the basic reference, L. DeLisle, *Le cabinet des manuscrits de la Bibliothèque Nationale*, Paris, II, 1874, pp. 142 ff.
27. Cf. a discussion of the meaning of "public" libraries in the Middle Ages in O. Thyregod, *Die Kulturfunktion der Bibliothek*, The Hague, 1936, pp. 7 ff.
28. M. P. Gilmore, *The World of Humanism*, New York, 1952, p. 186, for example.
29. D. Robathan, "Libraries of the Italian Renaissance," *Medieval Library*, ed. Thompson, pp. 519, 524.
30. M. Meiss, *Painting in Florence and Siena After the Black Death*, New York, 1964, pp. 78 ff.
31. I. Tassi, *Ludovico Barbo (1381-1443)*, Rome, 1952, p. 35.
32. T. Kaeppeli, *Inventari di libri di San Domenico di Perugia (1430-80)*, Rome, 1962, p. 14 note 5.
33. J. Moorman, *A History of the Franciscan Order*, Oxford, 1968, p. 490.
34. For Franciscan Observantism see I. da Milano, "San Bernardino da Siena e l'Osservanza minoritica," *S. Bernardino. Saggi e ricerche pubblicati nel quinto centenario della morte (1444-1944)*, Milan, 1944, pp. 379-406; I. Origo, *The World of San Bernardino*, New York, 1962, pp. 205 ff.; M. Heimbucher, *Die Orden und Kongregationen der katholischen Kirche*, Paderborn, I, 1933-1934, pp. 709 ff., *Ordini e congregazioni religiose*, ed. M. Escobar, Turin, I, 1951-1953, pp. 178 ff., Moorman, *passim.;* F. Antal, *Florentine Painting and its Social Background*, London, 1947, pp. 65 ff.
35. For Dominican Observantism see *Ordini e congregazioni*, I, pp. 402 ff., Heimbucher, *Die Orden*, I, pp. 490 ff.; Stefano Orlandi, *Il beato Lorenzo da Ripafratta*, Florence, 1956.
36. For the Congregation of S. Giustina see T. Lecciosotti, "La congregazione benedettina di S. Giustina e la riforma della chiesa al secolo XV," *Archivio della reale deputazione romana di storia patria*, LXVII, 1944, pp. 451-469; G. Penco, *Storia del monachesimo in Italia*, Rome, 1961, pp. 337 ff.; P. Sambin, *Ricerche di storia monastica medioevale*, Padua, 1959, pp. 69 ff.; Tassi, *Ludovico Barbo, passim.;* I Tassi, "La crisi della Congregazione di S. Giustina tra il 1419 e il 1431," *Benedictina*, V, 1951, pp. 55-111.
37. It became the Congregation of Monte Cassino (Congregazione cassinese) when it absorbed that cradle of the Benedictine Order after 1500.
38. A. della Torre, *Storia dell'accademia platonica di Firenze*, Florence, 1902, pp. 185 ff.
39. G. Uzielli, *La vita e i tempi di Paolo dal Pozzo Toscanelli*, Rome, 1894, pp. 54 ff.
40. G. Zippel, *Niccolò Niccoli*, Florence, 1890, pp. 66 ff.
41. Vespasiano, *Vite,* p. 10:

   Istando la sua Santità a Firenze . . . attendeva con ogni diligenza a riformare la Chiesa, e fare che i religiosi istessino a' termini loro, e di conventuali fargli osservanti, giusto alla possa sua. . . . riformò la sua Santità Santo Marco di Firenze . . . standovi dentro dieci o dodici frati, papa Eugenio lo riformò, e volle che Cosimo acconciasse quello luogo per i frati dell'osservanza di santo Domenico . . . Promise Cosimo alla sua Santità ispendervi dentro ducati diecimila, e andò a quarantamila.

   (My translation differs considerably from that given in Vespasiano, *Renaissance Princes, Popes, and Prelates*, trs. W. George and E. Waters, New York, 1963, p. 20.) Vespasiano goes on to list other houses, including the Badia in Florence, reformed by Eugene. Cf. L. Pastor, *The History of the Popes*, London, I, 1938, pp. 355-358.

42. For interpretations of Cosimo's aims see E. H. Gombrich, "The Early Medici as Patrons of Art," *Italian Renaissance Studies,* ed. E. F. Jacob, London, 1960, pp. 279 ff., and Antal, *Florentine Painting, passim.*

43. L. Sighinolfi, "La Biblioteca di Giovanni Marcanova," *Collectanea variae doctrinae Leoni S. Olschki,* Munich, 1921, pp. 187-222.

44. At least two fourteenth-century library spaces do survive. Two extant rooms at Assisi seem to be those in which the books were stored when an inventory of the collection was made in 1381, but they are apparently of little architectural interest (Cat. 1). The library installed in S. Maria Novella in Florence in 1338-1340 is preserved, but has been added to and altered many times (Cat. 25).

45. P. Egidi, "L'Abazia di S. Martino al Cimino presso Viterbo," *Rivista storica benedettina,* II, 1907, pp. 481 ff.

46. Humphreys, *Book Provisions,* pp. 56, 102-103. Humphreys frequently uses "shelves" when "desks" are clearly meant.

47. Cf. Lehmann, *Bibliotheksräume,* pp. 8 ff. Lehmann's term for the communal reference library is "gotische Studienbibliothek." He dates its appearance in Germany to the thirteenth century. See also W. Schürmeyer, *Bibliotheksräume aus fünf Jahrhunderten,* Frankfurt, a. M., 1929, p. 8.

48. R. Valturio bequeathed his collection of books to S. Francesco in Rimini (Cat. 48) in 1475 with the stipulation that the existing library be moved from ground level to more suitable quarters upstairs. See Thompson, *Medieval Library,* p. 559.

49. The desire for ample light, in addition to the need for dryness, was perhaps a minor factor in the elevation of the library above ground floor arcades.

50. Cf. the correspondence between Clement VII and Michelangelo concerning the design of the Laurentian Library in Florence (Cat. 22).

51. Other examples of libraries placed to the side of one cloister: Badia, Florence (Cat. 20; Fig. 13B); Monteoliveto Maggiore (Cat. 39; Fig. 13F); S. Lorenzo, Florence (Cat. 22); and SS. Annunziata, Florence (Cat. 19; Fig. 13A).

52. Examples of spinal libraries: S. Croce, Florence (Cat. 21; Fig. 32); S. Maria delle Grazie, Milan (Cat. 36; Fig. 13D); S. Vittore al Corpo, Milan (Cat. 37; Fig. 13E); S. Giovanni Evangelista, Parma (Cat. 44; Fig. 13G); S. Giovanni di Verdara, Padua (Cat. 42); S. Francesco, Cesena (Cat. 11); S. Agostino, Cremona (Cat. 14); and, probably, S. Barnaba, Brescia (Cat. 9); and S. Domenico, Ferrara (Cat. 17).

   Domenico Fontana has always been justly criticized for placing the Vatican Library of Sixtus V (1587) across the middle of Bramante's Cortile del Belvedere, and so dividing that huge, spatially cohesive courtyard into two smaller ones. But this location must have seemed obvious to him if he knew any of these earlier monastic libraries that separate cloisters. The interior of his library seems traditional as well, for it was a divided room of two instead of three aisles, and intended to house a manuscript collection. See Fontana, *Della trasportatione dell'-obelisco vaticano et delle fabriche di nostro signore Papa Sisto V,* Rome, I, 1590, pp. 82 ff.; Clark, *Care of Books,* pp. 49-50, 321-332; J. S. Ackerman, *The Cortile del Belvedere,* Vatican City, 1954, pp. 110-111.

53. J. Lipsius, *De Bibliothecis syntagma,* Antwerp, 1602 (English translation as Vol. V of *Literature of Libraries in the Seventeenth and Eighteenth Centuries,* eds. J. C. Dana and H. W. Kent, Chicago, 1907, pp. 95-96); Clark, *Care of Books,* p. 43.

54. Lipsius, p. 96.

54a. The adaptability of this structural form is best illustrated by recalling its frequent use in Renaissance *stable* design, for example, by Raphael at the Farnesina (Metropolitan Museum of Art, New York, 49.92.44; a sixteenth-century drawing), by Leonardo (Institute de France, Ms. B, fol. 31r), and so on. Its adaptability precludes any association with the ecclesiastical basilica.

55. C. Calzolai, *La storia della Badia a Settimo,* Florence, 1958, pp. 51 ff.

56. F. L. Del Migliore, *Firenze città nobilissima illustrata,* Florence, 1684, pp. 231 ff.; S. Orlandi, *Necrologio di S. Maria Novella,* Florence, 1955, I, xxii-xxiii and n. 19. The date given by Walter and Elisabeth Paatz in *Die Kirchen von Florenz* (Frankfurt a. M., 1940-1954, III, p. 699) is much too late.

57. Del Migliore, *Firenze,* pp. 231 ff. The account given by Paatz (II, pp. 2-10) is not reliable because it is based upon the inaccurate account given by E. Marzi, "La scuola di applicazione di sanità militare di Firenze e la sua sede," *Firenze (Rassegna mensile del Comune),* II, 1933, pp. 39-48.

58. This has already been pointed out by G. Morozzi, "Restauri nell'ex convento di S. Marco a Firenze," *Bolletino d'Arte,* IV, 1955, pp. 350-354. Other proposed sources for the quattrocento basilical library range from Fra Angelico's tiny predella *Presentation in the Temple* (ca. 1438) in

Cortona (A. Visani, "La biblioteca del convento di San Marco in Firenze," *L'Archiginnasio*, XXXV, 1940, p. 282; echoed by L. Gori-Montanelli, *Brunelleschi e Michelozzo*, Florence, 1957, p. 85) to the ancient Roman basilica (Paatz, III, p. 57, note 72), but such suggestions need not be taken seriously. The Cistercian connection already made by H. Willich (*Die Baukunst der Renaissance in Italien*, Berlin-Neubabelsberg, 1914, p. 126) was rejected by Paatz because Willich mentioned the Cistercian *library* and Paatz rightly could find none.

Those for whom quattrocento architecture is simply a Renaissance manifestation, and therefore derivable from antique sources, will question Michelozzo's use of a Gothic prototype. They must remember, however, that the ancient library as an architectural form was known to the quattrocento only from literary sources, and they are not very informative. Michelozzo's adaptation of the medieval columnar space for use as a monastic library might nonetheless have had some vague antique justification. Ancient descriptions of ancient libraries frequently mention colonnades. Thus the library of Lucullus is described by Plutarch as "open to every one; and in the adjoining colonnades and exedras learned Greeks were . . . made welcome" (Lipsius, p. 65), and Augustus's Octavian library near the Theater of Marcellus in Rome is mentioned by Dio Cassius thusly: "Augustus "built a colonnade and in it established a library . . ." (*ibid.*, p. 71). That such descriptions were not overlooked in the period under discussion is demonstrable from Francisco Albertini's reference to Hadrian's library as *"pulcherrimam marmoreis exornata colunis"* in his discussion of the ancient libraries of Rome (*Opusculus mirabilibus noue e ueteris urbis Rome*, Rome, 1515, fol. 51r). Also, Michelozzo's provision for a separate room for the Greek manuscripts, as well as Michelangelo's early project for the Laurentian in which a division into Latin and Greek collections was contemplated (Cat. 22), probably depends upon the similar arrangement of ancient libraries.

Such was the extent of the information available to the quattrocento on the architecture of the ancient library. The bulk of the descriptions of these ancient rooms provided by ancient authors treats of their decoration, including the use of portraits of famous writers and other heros (cf. Cat. 9).

59. The floor of the Pilgrim's Hall of the Badia a Settimo, on the Arno west of Florence, has been raised some eight feet above the original pavement as the result of flood deposits (Figs. 4-5).

60. L. H. Heydenreich, "Gedanken über Michelozzo di Bartolomeo," *Festschrift Wilhelm Pinder*, Leipzig, 1938, pp. 254-290.

61. As late as the 1540s Sansovino was still having trouble holding up a vault above the second floor reading room of his library in Venice (it fell during construction). This was in part due to the airiness of his sustaining arcades, as W. Lotz has pointed out ("The Roman Legacy in Sansovino's Venetian Buildings," *Journal of the Society of Architectural Historians*, XXII, 1963, p. 10), but the superimposition of vault above void is found in such earlier monastic libraries as S. Domenico in Bologna (Cat. 2) or S. Sepolcro in Piacenza (Cat. 47).

62. Excavations have shown that the library at Cesena was intended to be even longer.

63. R. Wittkower, "Michelangelo's Biblioteca Laurenziana," *Art Bulletin*, XVI, 1934, p. 146.

64. Scholars who used the monastic collections were apparently less particular than such collectors of "fine editions" as Federico da Montefeltro, in whose library at Urbino, according to Vespasiano da Bisticci (*Vite*, p. 213): *"non ve n'è ignuno [libro] a stampa, che se ne sarebbe vergògnato."* Printed works appear early in inventories of the collections of S. Domenico in Perugia (Cat. 45), the Badia in Florence (Cat. 20), and S. Domenico in Bologna (Cat. 2).

65. The effects of the invention of printing have recently been studied at length by R. Hirsch, *Printing, Selling and Reading 1450-1550*, Wiesbaden, 1967.

66. Cf. K. M. Setton, "From Medieval to Modern Library," *Proceedings of the American Philosophical Society*, 104, 1960, p. 381.

67. Chaytor, *From Script to Print*, pp. 18-19.

68. As C. F. Bühler has shown (*The Fifteenth Century Book*, Philadelphia, 1960, p. 16), there are some late fifteenth- and early sixteenth-century manuscripts that are actually hand copies of printed works.

69. A recent example is P. M. Wolf, "Michelangelo's Laurenziana and Inconspicuous Traditions," *Marsyas*, XII, 1964-1965, pp. 16 ff., in which the *ricetto* alone is discussed.

70. C. de Tolnay, *Michelangiolo*, Florence, 1951, p. 171. For a complete anthology of critical opinion about the Laurentian see G. Vasari, *La vita di Michelangelo*, ed. P. Barrochi, Milan, III, 1962, pp. 860 ff.

71. See note 54a.

72. J. S. Ackerman, *The Architecture of Michelangelo*, London, I, 1961, p. 34 (revised ed., Penguin Books, 1971, pp. 100 ff.).

II Catalogue

THE CATALOGUE LISTS only those monastic libraries erected between 1300 and 1600 for which I have found information of some architectural interest. Monasteries are arranged alphabetically by city. Names in square brackets designate totally destroyed libraries. Names in parenthesis designate significantly altered libraries. An asterisk denotes a library known to me only from published sources. Bibliographic references are listed chronologically, and are not repeated in the general bibliogaphy unless their scope goes beyond that of the specific entry.

KEY TO ABBREVIATED REFERENCES

Cecchini, 1960   Giovanni Cecchini, *6 biblioteche monastiche rinascimentali,* Milan, 1960.

Cecchini, 1967   Giovanni Cecchini, "Evoluzione architettonico-strutturale della biblioteca pubblica in Italia dal secolo XV al XVII," *Accademie e biblioteche d'Italia,* XXXV, 1967, pp. 27-47.

Clark   John Willis Clark, *The Care of Books,* Cambridge, 2d. ed., 1909.

Filarete   *Filarete's Treatise on Architecture,* tr. John R. Spencer, 2 vols., New Haven and London, 1965.

Gottlieb   Theodor Gottlieb, *Ueber mittelalterliche Bibliotheken*, Leipzig, 1890.

Gutiérrez, 1954   David Gutiérrez, "De antiquis ordinis eremitarum sancti augustini bibliothecis," *Analecta augustiniana*, XXIII, 1954, pp. 164-372.

Kaeppeli, 1955   Tommaso Kaeppeli, "La bibliothèque de Saint-Eustorge à Milan à la fin du XVe siècle," *Archivum fratrum praedicatorum*, XXV, 1955, pp. 5-74.

Kaeppeli, 1966   Tommaso Kaeppeli, "Antiche biblioteche domenicane in Italia," *Archivum fratrum praedicatorum*, XXXVI, 1966, pp. 5-80.

Laurent   M.-H. Laurent, *Fabio Vigili et les bibliothèques de Bologne au début de XVIe siècle*, Vatican City, 1943.

Morisani   Ottavio Morisani, *Michelozzo architetto*, Milan, 1951.

Paatz   Walter and Elisabeth Paatz, *Die Kirchen von Florenz*, Frankfurt a. M., 1940-1954.

Rotondi   Giuseppe Rotondi, "Fra Serafino Razzi e il suo viaggio in Lombardia nel 1572," *Archivio storico lombardo*, Ser. 6, LI, 1924, pp. 186-214.

Vasari   Giorgio Vasari, *Le vite più eccellenti pittori, etc.*, ed. Gaetano Milanesi, Florence, 1906.

Vespasiano   Vespasiano da Bisticci, *Vite di uomini illustri del secolo XV*, eds. Paolo D'Ancona and Erhard Aeschlimann, Milan, 1951.

1. **Assisi, S. Francesco.*

Mother house of the Franciscan Order erected after the death of the Founder.

An inventory of 1381 depicts a library divided into two parts: a "libraria publica" or reference collection, and a "libreria secreta" or stored lending collection. The reference library was a rectangular room running east and west with side windows and 181 volumes chained to two rows of nine reading desks each. This room seems to have survived, but is apparently of little architectural interest.

Bibliography: G. Fratini, *Storia della basilica e del convento di S. Francesco in Assisi,* Prato, 1882; Gottlieb, p. 181; G. Mazzatinti, *Inventorio dei manoscritti delle biblioteche d'Italia,* Forli, IV, 1894, pp. 21 ff.; L. Alessandri, *Inventario dell'antica biblioteca del s. convento di S. Francesco in Assisi compilato nel 1381,* Assisi, 1906; Clark, pp. 200-201.

2. *Bologna, S. Domenico.* Figs. 14C, 16-19.

The Dominican friary was established soon after the friars arrived in the city, 1218. *Studium Generale* by 1248. Seat of the Law Faculty of the University from the thirteenth century; unit of the Theological Faculty after 1364. Reformed 1427.

An inventory prior to 1381 depicts a room containing 472 volumes chained to 52 desks divided into two equal rows. Probably a hall about nine meters wide with exposed wooden trusses was located on the upper level of the wing south of and parallel to the church. Erected at an unknown date (fourteenth century?).

About 1440 the earlier building was showing signs of decay. For the following years there are records of repeated efforts to gather money sufficient to erect a new library, but the funds accumulated were frequently drained off for more pressing needs. A specific project must have been prepared by 1461, because a document of that year notes that materials assembled for the new library were needed elsewhere, and it seems logical that no materials would have been acquired unless a definite design had been established. In October 1464, demolition of parts of the old building began; the contract for the sixteen columns with capitals and bases is of May 1465. Actual construction of the library (after rebuilding the lower floor) began in April 1466, and the windows and reading desks were installed in 1469. The library has been restored recently.

Giovanni di Martino de'Rossi, called Giovanni Negro, appears in the documents as head of the *muratori* who built the library. Zucchini assigned the design of the entire building to him, but Alce gives him only the lower floor and exterior elevation. Pagno di Lapo, a Florentine follower of Michelozzo, designed the chapel of S. Antonio in the church, and this was erected under the patronage of Antonio Bonafè, a Florentine banker active in Bologna after the middle of the century, who also contributed to the library. Alce sees a stylistic difference between the "Tuscan" library and the "Bolognese" lower floor and exterior elevations, and suggests that Pagno was responsible for the former while Giovanni Negro designed the latter, and erected the entire building. He could be right, but the differences between upper and lower floors could also be accounted for by their different purposes, or the fact that the lower floor was *rebuilt,* whereas the library was a new design. It is difficult to imagine a design cut up the way Alce proposes. Either Pagno acted as a "consultant" on a "Tuscan" library for Giovanni Negro, or was responsible for the whole design that bears the marks of a compromise solution by a Tuscan architect working in a "provincial" atmosphere.

The new library occupies the site of the old, on the upper floor of the building south of and parallel to the church. The lower floor of this two-story brick building located between cloisters is divided by a row of stout octagonal brick piers into two aisles, like the lower floor of the building at Cesena (Cat. 11). But unlike Cesena the library is not centered on these lower aisles. It is shifted to one side, so that the piers are beneath the columns to the south, and the columns to the north rest upon the corresponding exterior wall of the lower floor. The north wall of the library rests upon the arcade of the first cloister; the south wall is continuous from the ground up.

Internally the library, 38.3 by 14.5 meters, is divided by two longitudinal rows of eight Composite columns each. Like the rooms at S. Marco in Florence (Cat. 23) and S. Francesco in Cesena, the bays of the side aisles are cross-vaulted while the central passage is covered from end to end by a continuous barrel vault. Relatively large windows centered in each bay of the side walls light the interior, which like Cesena is of a warm green tone. Unlike Cesena, however, this library is abundantly illuminated, and thus has a more expansive spatial effect, although this is due in part to the huge walls of glass that now open the room into later additions at either end, and in part to the absence of the original reading desks.

We have four old descriptions of this room that supplement our understanding of the present empty shell. In Novella fifty-seven of *Le Porretane* (finished 1478), Giovanni Sabadino degli Arienti relates that

L'è stata mia consuetudine . . . andare spesse volte a la libraria de S. Domenico nostro, dove stano li frati predicatori, degna e magnifica quanto forsi un'altra in Italia a quisti tempi se trovi, per studiare certe opere, le quale in altro luoco de la nostra cità non se trovano.

This is an explicit statement of the accessibility of this library to scholars outside of the cloister.

Fabio Vigili visited the monastery between 1510 and 1512, and left a partial inventory of its library. In this "nobili" and "insignis" room (adjectives he uses in reference to S. Domenico alone, although he visited many monastic libraries in the city), he found the books located on two rows of 32 reading desks each. But Vigili's count was either incomplete or incorrect, or two additional desks were added in the sixteenth century, for the description left by Fra Serafino Razzi (1572) gives a total of 66 desks. The library, he says,

di tre navi in volta, tutta tinto di verdi, è distinta in due parti, e la prima sotto chiave commune tiene 33 banchi per lato, e la 2ª sotto *chiave particolare contiene alcuni libri greci, e scritti a mano.*

The division of the library into two parts mentioned here is also noted in a seventeenth-century reference to the collection (Lomeier, *De bibliothecis*) in which 66 desks are located in an "outer room" and thirty-two are in an "inner one."

In 1496 a hall was added to the west end of the basilical library described above, the gift of Ludovico and Giovanna Bolognini. It was a necessary addition to a library housing an ever-expanding collection not only of manuscripts but of incunabula as well. This room was remodelled in the seventeenth century, and we can be certain of little else than that it was a hall with high straight walls and flat ceiling, and that it contained, at least in the early seventeenth century, the 32 desks mentioned by Lomeier.

Bibliography: G. S. degli Arienti, *Le Porretane*, ed. G. Gambarin, Bari, 1914, p. 361; *A Seventeenth-Century View of European Libraries. Lomeier's De Bibliothecis, Chapter X*, ed. and tr. J. W. Montgomery, Berkeley and Los Angeles, 1962, p. 18; Rotondi, p. 195; G. Zucchini, "Le librerie del convento di S. Domenico a Bologna," *Memorie domenicane*, 1936, pp. 199-208; 269-279; 1937, pp. 41-46, 80-90, 214-225; Laurent, pp. 11-107; Kaeppeli, 1955, p. 5; *La biblioteca di San Domenico in Bologna*, ed. M. Casali, Bologna, 1959; V. Alce and A. D'Amato *La biblioteca di S. Domenico in Bologna*, Florence, 1961 (the text is identical in the last two items; there are more and better illustrations in Casali); Cecchini, 1960, pp. 8-9; Cecchini, 1967, pp. 29-31.

3. [*Bologna, S. Francesco.*]

Franciscan friary and *Studium Generale* founded as early as 1223. Seat of the Arts Faculty of the University by the thirteenth century; unit of the Theological Faculty after 1364. Remained unreformed.

An inventory of the library made in 1421 lists 649 items without giving their location. The partial listing of Fabio Vigili (*ca.* 1510-12) lists 117 items stored on two rows of 13 and 18 desks.

Some monastic buildings remain, but it is doubtful that the quattrocento library still exists because a late eighteenth-century description of the convent now in the Archivio di Stato in Bologna mentions a library built in 1681. This must have replaced the older room.

Bibliography: Laurent, pp. xxxii-xxxiv, 108-121, 236-266.

4. * *Bologna, S. Giacomo Maggiore.*
   Monastery of the Austin Hermits. Unit of the Theological Faculty after 1364. Remained unreformed.
   Fabio Vigili's partial listing (*ca.* 1510-12) depicts a room with two rows, one of nine, the other of ten reading desks.

Bibliography: Laurent, pp. 122-136.

5. [*Bologna, S. Michele in Bosco.*]
   Fabio Vigili's incomplete inventory of the library of this Olivetan house (*ca.* 1510-12) lists 45 items on two rows of 21 reading desks each. Malaguzzi-Valeri mentions a library built in 1517 (replaced in seventeenth century).

Bibliography: F. Malaguzzi-Valeri, *La chiese e il convento di S. Michele in Bosco*, Bologna, 1895, pp. 33, 77 ff.; Laurent, pp. 137-143.

6. * *Bologna, S. Paolo in Monte.*
   Observant Franciscan friary founded 1417. Fabio Vigili's incomplete listing mentions 92 works on two rows of nine reading desks each.

Bibliography: Laurent, pp. 144-156.

7. * *Bologna, S. Procolo.*
   The Benedictine monastery was joined to the Congregation of S. Giustina in 1436 when the rebuilding of the neglected church and convent was begun. Rebuilt again in sixteenth century. Fabio Vigili depicts a library stored in a room with two rows of desks, 11 desks per row. He visited the monastery between 1510 and 1512.

Bibliography: Laurent, pp. 157-161; M. Fanti, *San Procolo*, Bologna, 1963, pp. 116 ff., 222 ff.

8. * *Bologna, S. Salvatore.*
According to Frati, who gives no source, this library, finished in 1522, was

un'ampia sala che trovavasi a metà del dormitorio . . . La soffitta era tutta in legno a spartimenti ottangolari, che avevano nel mezzo un rosone dorato, circondato d'arabeschi a chiaro scuro. Tali spartimenti erano disposti in quattro linei, collegate de travi per lungo e per traverso, *ognuna delle quali nel mezzo era ornata d'un rosone dorto e nel rimanente di anella intrecciate a due ordini. I libri erano anticamente disposti su banchi e vi erano fermati con catenelle . . . Ma nel 1635 ai vecchi banchi furono sostituiti gli armarj di noce.*

This would certainly have been a hall-type library. An inventory of *ca.* 1533 lists 581 items without location; Fabio Vigili's list of *ca.* 1510-12 mentions only nine benches. Earlier inventories of 1322 and 1429 are mentioned by Gottlieb.

Bibliography: L. Frati, "La biblioteca dei Canonici Regolari di S. Salvatore di Bologna," *Rivista delle biblioteche,* II, 1889, p. 2; Gottlieb, p. 185; Laurent, pp. xxxiv-xxxvii, 266-347.

9. *Brescia, S. Barnaba.* Figs. 20, 22-23.
The Austin Hermit monastery of S. Barnaba was founded in the late thirteenth century, and joined the Observant branch of the Order in 1456. It was suppressed in 1797.

Contained within the later buildings of the Scuola T. Speri is a fifteenth-century room always described as the old library of S. Barnaba. Although I have seen no specific documentary proof of this, and the collection of books is unknown, the frescoes decorating the four walls of the room certainly suggest its original use as a library. It is on the upper floor of a building to the south of and parallel to the seventeenth-century church. Its date of erection is usually given as 1490, when the city donated 90 ducats for a library here, but Ferrari recently assigned the frescoes by Giovan Pietro da Cemmo to the period 1486-1490 on the basis of style.

The room is a simple, broad rectangular hall, 24.5 by 10.87 meters, with a decorated, coved wooden ceiling divided into rectangular panels by latticework. Five regularly spaced rectangular windows open each of the long sides. All four walls are divided by a painted architecture of socle, frieze, and the intervening pilaster order, and illuminated with allegories on the end walls and portrait tondi on the side walls, all relating to the Order of Austin Hermits.

There exists no study of library decoration in the quattrocento, nor do I include it in this work. But I would like to point out the curious similarity between the architectural organization of the side walls here, and those of an ancient Roman library discovered on the Esquiline by R. A. Lanciani (Fig. 21). I find this curious because to my knowledge no ancient libraries were recognized as such in the fifteenth and sixteenth centuries.

Bibliography: L. F. Fè d'Ostiani, *Storia tradizione e arte nelle vie di Brescia*, Brescia, 2d ed., 1927, pp. 139-146; A. Morassi, *Brescia (Catalogo delle cose d'arte e di antichità d'Italia)*, Rome, 1939, pp. 80-82; M. L. Ferrari, *Giovan Pietro da Cemmo*, Milan, 1956, pp. 67 ff.; *Storia di Brescia*, ed. G. T. degli Alfieri, Brescia, II, 1963, pp. 691-692.

10. [*Brescia, S. Domenico.*]

Fra Serafino Razzi saw in 1572 a library "di 12 banchi per lato" in this Dominican house. The church was built between 1609 and 1615 by Pietro Maria Bagnadore (1545/50-1619?). He may also have designed the monastery which existed until a few years ago. It contained a basilical space on the upper floor of the wing to the south-west of the large cloister. If this was a library erected around 1600, it must have replaced the room described by Razzi. Unfortunately no record of its function has yet come to light.

Bibliography: Rotondi, p. 211; L. F Fè d'Ostiani, *Storia tradizione e arte nelle vie di Brescia*, Brescia, 2d ed., 1927, pp. 84-89; Kaeppeli, 1955, p. 6; *Storia di Brescia*, ed. G. T. degli Alfieri, Brescia, II, 1963, p. 875.

11. *Cesena, S. Francesco (Biblioteca Malatestiana).* Figs. 14B, 24-28.

This library was part of a Franciscan friary founded in the thirteenth century. By the mid-fourteenth the friary had become the seat of a *studium* with a collection of books, and by 1445 there was need for a building to house the expanding collection. The surviving room was erected between 1447 and 1452 under the aegis of the local tyrant, Malatesta Novello. A fifteenth-century plaque to the right of the entrance tells us that the architect was Matteo Nuti. This is his masterwork.

Although physically part of a friary that contained a school, the Malatestian Library was not administratively a monastic library. Malatesta in 1461 gave the Comune an interest in running the library, and that fact alone has preserved it nearly intact, with its original collection of books, and its original furnishings. As a secularly administered collection, it escaped the spoliation of monastic property under Napoleon, and survived the destruction of the church and the remainder of the friary in the nineteenth century. It is the sole quattrocento monastic library in which the original furnishings were retained; only the cinquecento Laurentian in Florence rivals it in this respect.

The library, 40.85 by 10.4 meters, is located on the second floor of a two-story brick building with gable roof that originally stood at a right angle to the church, and between two cloisters. The lower floor, older than the library above, is a vaulted space of two aisles separated by piers. The library above is a basilical space divided into three aisles by two rows of ten free-standing, fluted columns surmounted by curious capitals bearing the many Malatesta arms. The piers below and the columns above are not aligned. The narrower central aisle of the library is surmounted by a continuous barrel vault, while there are series of cross vaults above the side aisles. Engaged brick half-columns corresponding to the free-standing columns divide the side walls into bays. Light enters symmetrically from both long sides through series of relatively small but numerous (two per bay) arched openings. These admit a soft light that suffuses the space but only slightly illuminates it. The walls retain their original warm green color.

Each side aisle contains 29 wooden reading desks, each composed of a sloping surface upon which to rest a book while it is being read, and a lower shelf for the storage of the books that are chained in place.

Bibliography: G. M. Muccioli, *Catalogus Codicum Manuscriptorum Malatestianae Caesenatis Bibliotheque,* Cesena, 1780-1784; Clark, pp. 193 ff.; A. Campana, "Origine, formazione e vicende della Malatestiana," *Accademie e biblioteche d'Italia,* XXI, 1953, pp. 3-16; "La biblioteca malatestiana in Cesena," *L'Architettura,* IV, 1959, pp. 704-709; Cecchini, 1960, pp. 6-7; A. Domeniconi, *La Biblioteca malatestiana,* Udine, 1962; Cecchini, 1967, pp. 28-29.

12. [*Como, S. Giovanni Battista*].

In 1572 Fra Serafino Razzi saw in this convent a "bella" library with "13 banchi per lato." There appears to be no monastery of this name presently in the city.

Bibliography: Rotondi, p. 210; Kaeppeli, 1955, p. 6.

13. (*Crema, S. Agostino.*)

A hall 16.4 by 9.3 meters with exposed beams on the upper level off what was the dormitory of this ex-monastery is said to have been the library. Neither the date of its erection nor its original contents are known. Now part of the Centro Culturale S. Agostino.

Bibliography: W. T. de Gregory, *Fra Agostino da Crema,* Crema, 1950, pp. 61-66; M. L. Ferrari, *Giovan Pietro da Cemmo,* Milan, 1956, p. 13.

14. [*Cremona, S. Agostino.*]

This Austin Hermit monastery dated back to the thirteenth century; its book collection had reached significant proportions by the middle of the fourteenth. Although destroyed at the beginning of the last century in the wake of the Napoleonic suppression of the religious Orders this late sixteenth-century library can be reconstructed from contemporary descriptions. The oldest of these, contained on ff. 163r-171v of Ms. 331 in the Biblioteca Angelica in Rome, has been published in full by Gutiérrez. The phrase *"Pur hora, che siamo nell'anno 1599"* dates the description to a period before the room was totally finished. It was begun in 1589 (the date 1517 given by Aglio and others seems to stem from a mis-read inscription).

The description depicts a basilical space (of special form) on the upper floor of a two-story building dividing two cloisters. The columns above are centered upon the walls of a corridor below. Both floors are vaulted. The library itself, 28 by 72 *braccia,* is entered from the end of a long dormitory through a foyer (*bochirale*), eight by eight *braccia,* located between flanking monks' cells. Rectangular windows of two sizes were placed in the long side walls. Small windows, two by three *braccia,* are placed above larger ones, five by three *braccia;* there are five pairs of windows per side. These are spaced 11 *braccia* apart, and six and a half *braccia* from the end walls. The windows are filled with thick transparent glass set in a pattern of lozenges and variously sized squares, with bronze armatures, and the device of the Austin Hermits painted and fired on each one.

These window units are covered by cross vaults that alternate with what seems to be a special kind of barrel vault (*una volta a facie*). The vaulting rests upon a terra cotta architrave sustained by 24 columns of Veronese marble, dappled red and white and highly polished. The capitals vary from Composite to Ionic to Doric. These columns are divided into two rows of 12 each, but they are also paired, so that in each row there are six pairs of columns, an arrangement described as *"tal forma et ordine moderna."* The pairs are said to be nine *braccia* apart and within each pair the columns are spaced three *braccia,* but these dimensions cannot be made to fit the overall dimensions of the room, or the window (and therefore the vault) spacing.

Walls and vaults are brightly frescoed with simulated architecture and allegorical figures pertaining to the subjects collected in 16 book presses set against the walls beneath the barrel (?) vaults. The collection is divided into 16 parts: Greek, Latin, and Vernacular Grammar; Rhetoric and Logic; Philosophy; Old Testament; New Testament; Doctors of the Church; Scholasts; Canon Law; Civil Law; Crime (*la facoltà criminale*); Mathematics; Military Science; Medicine; Natural History; Commerce; History and miscellaneous. The book presses, each of which holds some 500 volumes on shelves behind doors, are specifically described as something new and superior to the old reading desks:

lasciando da parte quelle scanzie de libri incatenati che occupavano delle tre parti le due di vasi della libreria, habbiamo ritrovato nouva inventione de credenzoni per la conserva de libri.

These presses are four and a half *braccia* high, one and a third deep, and vary from eight to five *braccia* wide depending upon their placement in the room.

A second description was discussed by Novati who is quoted in Gutiérrez. It agrees in general with that summarized here, but adds the information that the central aisle was wider than the side aisles. These descriptions permit us to reconstruct a library room in which the traditional basilical space has been slightly updated by the use of paired columns, an elaborate vaulting system, rich materials, carvings, frescoes, and presses instead of reading desks.

Luigi Crema informs me by letter that the columns from this library were re-used in the courtyard of the Palazzo Trecchi in Cremona, remodeled at the beginning of the nineteenth century.

Bibliography: G. Aglio, *Le pitture e le sculture della città di Cremona,* Cremona, 1794, pp. 111-112; L. Manini, *Memorie storiche della città di Cremona,* Cremona, II, 1819-1820, pp. 57-59; F. Novati, "La biblioteca degli Agostiniani di Cremona," *Il Bibliofilo,* IV, 1883, pp. 27-29, 54-56; L. Luchini, "Le pitture della biblioteca di S. Agostino in Cremona ora distrutta," *Arte e storia,* XXI, 1902, pp. 142-144; A. Sorbelli, *Inventari dei manoscritti delle biblioteche d'Italia,* Florence, LXX, 1939, pp. x ff.; V. C. Dainotti, *La biblioteca governativa nella storia della cultura cremonese,* Cremona, 1946, pp. 62-63; M. Monteverdi, *La chiesa di S. Agostino,* Cremona, 1953, p. 8; D[avid] G[utiérrez], "La biblioteca agostiniana di Cremona alla fine del secolo XVI," *Analecta augustiniana,* XXIV, 1961, pp. 313-330.

15. [*Cremona, S. Domenico.*]

The library in this Dominican convent was rebuilt in 1576 as a basilical space divided by Doric columns.

Bibliography: P. Merula, *Santuario di Cremona,* Cremona, 1627, p. 204; P. M. Domaneschi, *De rebus coenobii cremonensis ordinis praedicatorum . . .* , Cremona, 1767, p. 53; L. Manini, *Memorie storiche della città di Cremona,* Cremona, II, 1819-1820, pp. 60-63; V. C. Dainotti, *La biblioteca governativa nella storia della cultura cremonese,* Cremona, 1946, pp. 61-62; Kaeppeli, 1966, p. 13.

16. * *Faenza, S. Andrea (S. Domenico).*

Serafino Razzi visited this monastery in 1572:

[*La libreria*] *posta in luogo commodo, cioè nel mezzo de dormitorij, con vaghe pitture adorna, e con pareti tinte di verde, tiene ventun banco per lato. Et intesta di lei si vede dipinto un san Tommaso in cattedra che legge, con questo verso latino sopra "Cui dant angelicum divina volumina nomen."*

The manuscript *Liber Consiliorum Conventus S. Andrae* now in the Biblioteca Communale in Faenza provides some information about the history of the library here. Construction was going on between 1459 and 1460, but the room built then was either replaced or enlarged in 1493 when Pagno di Lapo Protigiani was commissioned to make ten columns for the (basilical?) library. The library was decorated between 1508 and 1510.

Bibliography: Rotondi, 195; Kaeppeli, 1955, p. 6; C. Grigioni, "Il Duomo di Faenza," *L'Arte,* XXVI, 1923, p. 173; C. Grigioni, *La Pittura faentina,* Faenza, 1935, pp. 227, 291-292, 309-312, 331; P. Zama, *Gli archivi delle congregazioni religiose,* Faenza, 1946, pp. 51-53; Kaeppeli, 1966, pp. 15-16.

17. [*Ferrara, S. Domenico.*]

S. Domenico was the seat of the Arts Faculty of the local University. Documents cited by Cecchini indicate the presence of a library here in the late fourteenth century. Another was erected in the early decades of the sixteenth century, and was described by Guarini as

una copiosa libraria in tre navi distinta, da convenevoli colonne di marmo, ivi reposte dalla pietà d'alcuni nobili Cittadini, le cui armi, in esse si veggono scolpite, la quale in se contiene vent'otto banchi per parte, tutti ben provveduti di numerosa quantità di . . . Libri . . . lasciativi dal dottissimo Celio Calcagnini [1479-1541] . . . sopra la Porta della detta Libraria stà sepoltro [Calcagnini], in un magnifico deposito di marmo, comme dalle qui sotto notate inscri-

zioni si legge in esso incise. QUUM CAELIUS CALCAGNINUS NIHIL MAGIS OPTA-VERIT VIVENS, QUAM DE OMNIBUS PRO FORTUNAE CAPTU QUAM OPTIME MERERI: DECEDENS BIBLIOTECAM, IN QUA MULTO MAXIMAM AETATIS PARTEM EGIT, IN SUORUM CIVIUM GRATIAM PUBLICARI, IN EA SE CONDI MANDAVIT . . . ANNO SAL. MDXL.

North of the present church, at ground level of a building which once separated two cloisters, is a rectangular room divided into three aisles by two rows of eight columns resting upon pedestals. The structure above the capitals is recent. Muratori has identified this room as the Biblioteca Calcagnini, and Cecchini concurred in this identification, but it seems very unlikely that any library erected near the Po (which was closer to the city then than it is now) would have been placed at ground level. The existing room may have been a dormitory beneath the basilical library, but the library itself has certainly disappeared.

Bibliography: M. Guarini, *Compendio historico dell'origine . . . delle chiese . . . di Ferrara,* Ferrara, 1621, p. 90; G. Muratori, "Le tombe di Giovan Battista e Giulio Canani in S. Domenico e la biblioteca dell'attiguo omonimo convento . . . ," *Gazzetta Padana,* January 31, 1961; *idem,* "Il restaurando S. Domenico e la scuola medici di Ferrara," *Gazzetta Padana,* September 30, 1961; *idem,* "Monumenti di storia dell'Università di Ferrara," *Atti dell'accademia delle scienze di Ferrara,* 40, 1963; Cecchini, 1967, pp. 34-35.

18. * *Fiesole, Badia.*

Lateran Canonry rebuilt after 1456 by Cosimo de'Medici. Vespasiano tells us that he stocked the library with 200 volumes produced by 45 scribes in 22 months.

Avogadro's description of this library is fantastic. According to him it had an entrance of gilt marble crowned with a figure of Apollo playing the lyre as the Muses dance. Beyond this was a brass threshold, ivory doors, gilt beams, windows of crystal set in silver, richly decorated walls, books chained with silver chains and bound in gold. Despite all of this the actual library here, a small square room on the second floor above the *stanza del fuoco,* seems to be of little architectural interest.

Bibliography: Vespasiano, pp. 28, 413-415; Filarete, I, fol. 189v; V. Viti, *La Badia fiesolana,* Florence, 1926; E. H. Gombrich, "Alberto Avogadro's Description of the Badia of Fiesole . . . ," *Italia medioevale e umanistica,* V, 1962, pp. 217-229.

19. (*Florence, SS. Annunziata.*) Figs. 13A, 29-31.

This was a Servite house founded in 1250. We first hear of a collection of books in the early fourteenth century. A document of 1339 specifically mentions a library, but there is no indication of its location or appearance.

The midfifteenth-century rebuilding of the church and monastery, a documented work by Michelozzo, included a new library erected between 1450 and 1455 (documents in Taucci, 1935-1936). Despite the date of erection, Marchini suggested that this library was probably conceived as early as the mid-1430s. He could be right, since that would put this unvaulted hall prior to Michelozzo's revolutionary design (1438 ff.) for the library of S. Marco in Florence (Cat. 23), and more nearly contemporary to the similar room at S. Croce in Florence (Cat. 21), presumably also designed by Michelozzo. The library wing at SS. Annunziata was divided vertically into two floors of monks' cells in 1573, but its original appearance has been reconstructed in remarkable detail by Taucci from the many surviving documents and the existing fabric.

The library was located on the upper floor of the building on the south side of the first cloister, above the *foresteria,* and overlooking the piazza in front of the church and Brunelleschi's portico for the Ospedale degli Innocenti. It can be seen to the left of the church in a detail of the *Annunciation* painted in 1514 by Ridolfo Ghirlandaio in the Cappella dei Priori in the Palazzo Vecchio, where it is marked, as it still is, by a series of late Gothic *bifore.* Another view of it, from the west, is shown in a drawing of SS. Annunziata made just after 1500 by Fra Bartolomeo (Uffizi 45P). A third contemporary picture, from the south, is provided in a view of the convent in the Codex Rustichi.

The original room was a high open space with exposed, painted trusses above desks and benches. There were 31 desks and 58 benches, figures which would equal two rows of 15 and 16 desks each, with benches to either side. The end desks were placed flat against the end walls. The space was lighted through both long walls by series of tall *bifore* which, although most were closed in the sixteenth-century remodelling, remain a marked feature of the monastery, and a surprisingly "old-fashioned" design for a follower of Brunelleschi. A document of 1455 mentions "eighteen windows and nine eyes," and this would account for nine *bifore* with lancets surmounted by an oculus as in the present windows. [This did not account for all the windows, since there are still five in each side, and the Fra Bartolomeo view shows two more (the one on the right already closed) in the west end of the library.] The Rustichi view shows no windows in the east end (Taucci miscounted the windows; Paatz was misled by the Gothic design of these windows and dated them to the fourteenth century. His discussion should be used with caution.)

Bibliography: R. Taucci, "Delle biblioteche antiche dell'ordine e dei loro cataloghi," *Studi storici sull'Ordine dei Servi di Maria,* II, 1935-1936, pp. 145 ff.; R. Taucci, "La chiesa e il convento della SS. Annunziata di Firenze e i loro ampliamenti fino alla metà del secolo XV," *Studi storici sull'Ordine dei Servi di Maria,* IV, 1942, pp. 99-126; G. Marchini, "Aggiunte a Michelozzo," *La Rinascita,* VII, 1944, pp. 24-51, esp. p. 32 note 2; Paatz, I, p. 89; Morisani, pp. 91-92; L. Gori-Montanelli, *Brunelleschi e Michelozzo,* Florence, 1957, pp. 103 ff.

20. [*Florence, Badia.*] Fig. 13B.

The Benedictine abbey in Florence was founded in the tenth century, but by the end of the fourteenth it had fallen upon hard days: the thirteenth-century church was used as a stable. In 1415 the members of the abbey joined the reformed Congregation of S. Giustina, left it again in 1428, and rejoined in 1441. The revival of the abbey was begun under the direction of the Portuguese Abbot Gomes Ferreira da Silva (1419-1439). The library was founded when the humanist Antonio Corbinelli donated nearly 280 Greek and Latin manuscripts. Corbinelli's will is dated 1421; it was confirmed in 1424, a year before his death. The books did not go immediately to the abbey, but were there by 1439.

The arrival of these books coincides with a building campaign of the mid- and late 1430s that saw the erection of the Chiostro degli Aranci, with dormitory, stairs, and chapter room. But the documents from this time (which are incomplete) do not mention a library.

There is an early sixteenth-century inventory of the library at the Badia, published by Blum, which lists 754 manuscripts and 141 printed works. Apparently not all of these were in the library. The inventory is divided into three parts, and only the books listed in the second part are described as being on reading desks. These, 352 manuscripts and 129 printed works, were stored on 30 desks divided into two equal rows, one *"ex parte orientis,"* the other *"ex parte occidentis."*

Although this room was destroyed in the seventeenth century, we know it in some detail from a description written by Puccinelli, who actually saw it:

Don Ignatio Squarcialupi si ritorno al gouerno di questo suo Monastero nell'anno 1504, fabbricò la Libraria sopra del Capitolo vecchio con vaga, e bell'Architettura con Colonne, Capitelli, Pilastri, e fregi di pietra viua con vaghissime Pitture, riempiendola di molti Libri, parte de quali (nel tirarla à terra l'anno 1630, per fare la Sacristia nuoua) si sono smarriti, e persi.

From this description, together with the information contained in the inventory cited above, we can guess that the building was a basilical space (a hall would not contain "Colonne") with internal columns and pilasters, and a central passage between lateral rows of reading desks. The long axis of this room ran north and south, and it was above the old Chapter Room. Since the door and windows of the latter are preserved in the exterior wall of the present Sacristy on the east side of the Chiostro degli Aranci, there can be no doubt about the exact location of this early sixteenth-century library.

Bibliography: P. Puccinelli, *Cronica dell'insigne ed imperial'abbadia di Fiorenza,* Milan, 1664, p. 70; G. B. Uccelli, *Della Badia fiorentina,* Florence, 1858; U. Middledorf and W. Paatz, "Die gotische Badia zu Florenz . . . ," *Mitteilungen des kunsthistorischen Institutes in Florenz,* III, 1919-1932, pp. 502-503; P. Sanpaolesi, "Construzioni del primo quattrocento nella Badia fiorentina," *Rivista d'Arte,* XXIV, 1942, pp. 143-179; M. Tyszkiewicz, "Il chiostro degli Aranci della Badia fiiorentina," *Rivista d'Arte,* XXVII, 1951-1952, pp. 203-209; R. Blum, *La biblioteca della Badia fiorentina e i codici di Antonio Corbinelli,* Vatican City, 1951.

21.   (*Florence, S. Croce.*) Figs. 32-34.

This was a Franciscan Conventualist (unreformed) house dating back to St. Francis himself. The book collection here is at least as old as the midfourteenth century.

The fourteenth-century (?) library, of unknown appearance, burned with the rest of the monastery in 1423. The dormitory south of the Pazzi Chapel and east of the "Second Cloister" was rebuilt in the following years at the expense of the Comune. Michelozzo, according to Vasari, began to rebuild the Novitiate, behind Brunelleschi's Pazzi Chapel (1429 ff.), for the Medici during the 1440s. The library was replaced after 1427 by the Arte di Calimala with unrestricted funds left to it by an obscure, but obviously very wealthy, butcher named Michele di Guardino. Despite the four patrons (Pazzi, Medici, Comune, and Arte di Calimala), Saalman has suggested, convincingly I think, that with the exception of the Chapel, the entire project (Novitiate, dormitory, and library) must have been conceived as a whole, and must therefore be attributed to Michelozzo on the basis of Vasari's account.

A fifteenth-century inventory of the collection published by Mazzi reveals that the church stood on one side of the library and a cloister on the other, and that the long axis of the room was parallel to the church. This exactly fits the location of the library shown in the painted aerial view of the complex (1718) in the Museo del Opera of S. Croce. It was, then, in the existing building separating the two present cloisters, and was undoubtedly on the upper floor, for the Cappella dei Cerchi existed at ground level at the west of the same block, and in fact dictated the width of the building erected after 1427.

Without a thorough archaeological investigation of the existing structure, the exact appearance of the fifteenth-century room cannot be determined, because the room was thoroughly remodelled in the late eighteenth century. Richa, who saw it before that remodelling (but not certainly in its original form), describes it as

una Libreria ricca di rarissimi Libri tutti in cartapecora distribuiti in 60. banchi, essendo stata fabbricata da Michele della Famiglia de'Guardini . . . Questa Libreria ha la Porta nel Dormentorio si sopra, dove le Pitture che si veggono sono di Cosimo Ulivelli. . . .

The fact that Richa mentions Michele suggests that he had seen the original room, but his count of the reading desks differs from the precise information given in the fifteenth-century inventory, which lists 785 manuscripts chained to two rows of 35 desks each. It may be significant, however, that Richa mentions no columns, always a marked feature of a basilical library. My own brief inspection of the roof trusses that remain in place above the eighteenth-century ceiling led me to believe that this library, like that certainly by Michelozzo at SS. Annunziata (Cat. 19), was originally a hall with exposed trusses overhead. Only the fact that similar trusses exist above the masonry of the basilical room at Cesena (Fig. 25) leaves the question in slight doubt. If the fifteenth-century library was a hall, and encompassed the entire upper floor of the wing between cloisters, then it was a room approximately 40 by 8.5 meters.

The room was completely remodeled under the Grand Duke Pietro Leopoldo in 1770. After the suppression of the monastery in 1866, and the building of the adjacent Biblioteca Nationale Centrale, this space was used, ironically, only as a neglected storage area for the national collection.

Bibliography: G. Richa, *Notizie . . . delle chiese fiorentine,* I, pp. 110-111; F. Moisè, *Santa Croce di Firenze,* Florence, 1845, pp. 301 ff.; C. Mazzi, "L'Inventario quattrocentestico della biblioteca di S. Croce in Firenze," *Rivista delle biblioteche e degli archivi,* VIII, 1897, pp. 16-31, 99-113, 129-147; M. Bihl, "Ordinationes Fr. Bernardi De Guasconibus . . . Pro Bibliotheca Conventus S. Crucis, Florentina, An. 1356-1367," *Archivum franciscanum historicum,* 26, 1933, pp. 141-164; Paatz, I, p. 508 (mislocates library); H. Saalman, "Michelozzo Studies," *Burlington Magazine,* CVIII, May 1966, pp. 242 f.

22. *Florence, S. Lorenzo.* Figs. 35-37.

Built to house the Medici collection of manuscripts that had descended to Pope Clement VII from Lorenzo il Magnifico, the library at S. Lorenzo was being discussed as early as June, 1519, according to the memoirs of the Prior of the canonry, Giovan Battista Figiovanni. The reading room was designed by Michelangelo as an addition to the complex begun by Brunelleschi and Michelozzo in the previous century. It is a long narrow hall, 46.2 by 10.54 meters, entered through the famous *ricetto* with its monumental stairway. Construction was begun in the summer of 1524, but the library was not opened until 1571. It was erected on top of two existing floors of canon's apartments by strengthening the lower, older walls with a system of buttressing arcades. The library is located in the west wing of the cloisters, adjacent to the left transept of Brunelleschi's church.

A unique series of documents has been preserved concerning the design of this room that permits us to trace its evolution almost step by step. This documentation has been discussed many times, so I can be selective in the following review, although I do not always agree with previous writers. My interest is in the reading room only.

A design for the library is mentioned in a letter to Michelangelo from his agent in Rome, Giovanfrancesco Fattucci, dated December 30, 1523. From a letter of January 2, 1524 it becomes clear that the first design was for a library comprising two divisions: one for the Latin books, and one for the Greek works. In the second letter Michelangelo is asked for a design in his own hand, and in an undated reply to Fattucci's letter of January second, he indicates that he does not know where the library is to be placed (*"Io non ò notizia nessuna, nè so dove se la voglia fare"*). The design mentioned in these letters has been lost, but it is certain that it could not have been a vaulted, basilical design, because Fattucci's letter of January 30, 1524 reports that the Pope wants a vaulted library (*"desiderrebbe, che ella fussi in uolta di sopra come di sotto, per conto del fuoco che potrebbe uenire da tetti"*). This letter of January 30 mentions a plan of the canonry that is preserved in the Casa Buonarroti on two drawings (CB 10v and CB 9v) that were originally one. The library is shown in two different locations on this plan, and the letter expresses a preference for the one on the south side of the cloister (*"si diriza affare quella che è uolta a mezodi"*). Neither library shown on this plan was to be vaulted, so the Pope asks for a vaulted design. He believes that it will be necessary to destroy four rooms on each of the two floors of the existing monastery that will be beneath the library, and he asks that Michelangelo's assistant, Stefano, make a drawing to show exactly what was to be placed below the proposed site of the library on the south side of the cloister. Fattucci's letter of February 9, 1524 indicates that the Pope had received Stefano's drawing, which shows not four plus four rooms to be demolished, but seven plus seven rooms, if the site to the south of the cloister were going to be used. The Pope is unhappy with this development, and suggests using the alternate location shown on CV 10v plus CB 9v, that is, the site overlooking the piazza in front of the church ("*quella liberia che ua in sula piaza e inuerso il borgo Santo Lorenzo*"). He asks for information about the demolition that would be required to use this site. The next significant document is Fattucci's letter of March 10, 1954. He mentions that he had received from Michelangelo two plans of the library, and had shown them to the Pope, who, in turn, directed that the one next to the piazza be built ("*essi diritto a fare quella di verso la piazza*"). The letter indicates that it is longer than the other, and that the Pope is a little uneasy about the stair required to reach the library. Apparently any site chosen would have required the use of an entrance stair. We first hear of a design for a ceiling in this letter, so the Pope apparently had given up his demand for a library vaulted overhead, although he still insisted on vaults beneath the library. He asks for a design with two *studietti* for rare books, and a window at the end of the room ("*in capo le Libreria*"). He wants to know what such a window would overlook ("*orti o tetti o stalle*"). The alternate plan mentioned in this letter of March 10 could have been a proposal by Michelangelo for a site other than that selected by the Pope, because in the next letter, of April 3, 1524, Clement tells him to put the library where he wants, and that is next to the Old Sacristy ("*faciate la libreria doue uolete, et cioe siano le camere de uerso la sacrestia uechia*"), which is the present site. The Pope then requested a design showing the stair and the *studietti* (now increased to four), and repeated his request for vaults beneath the library to isolate it from the danger of fire from below ("*uorebe, che le camere sotto la libreria fussino fatte in uolta, acioche qualche inbriaco, come potrebe acadere fra preti, non metessi fuoco in camera e dalla camera in libreria*"). On April 13, 1524 Fattucci writes that the Pope is troubled because he does not want to rebuild the entire canonry just to add the library. With the definitive location established in the letter of April 3, Michelangelo submitted a plan for a cruciform library. The Pope liked it, and gave Michelangelo permission to encroach upon the courtyard ("*pigliate quelle noue braccia di corte che uoi auete disegniato, et cosi la crociera con quello graticolato che u'è segniato*"). On April 29, 1524 Fattucci acknowledges receipt of a new drawing. The Pope liked the idea of using barrel vaults (apparently above the lower apartments), but did not like to see the walls thickened by more than one *braccio,* since they have nothing to carry but the roof. In Fattucci's letter of May 13, 1524 Michelangelo is complimented upon his solution to this structural problem. He had proposed a system of internal-external buttresses to take the load of the added library without unnecesarily increasing the size of the old walls, or destroying more of the existing lower structure than necessary. A letter of July 9, 1524 directs the beginning of the work; that of August 2, 1524 relays the Pope's order not to begin the *crociera,* but to proceed in such a way as to make it possible to add it at a later date. It was, of course, never built. This letter also inquires about the long dimension of the library including an addition at the end and also about the number of benches to be placed in the room; it stipulates that the distance between them should be identical to that found in the library at S. Marco in Florence (Cat. 23). The Pope also wanted to know how many books could be stored in each desk. Fattucci's letter of October 1, 1524 suggests that the beginning raw construction had upset the Prior, Figiovanni, to such a degree that he has complained to the Pope that it looks like a dovecote (*"dice al papa, che uoi fate la libreria in colombaia"*). The letter of April 12, 1525 indicates that the addition mentioned on August 2, 1524 was to be made into a rare book room. Michelangelo's design for it is accepted on November 10. It was to be built as designed, but of course it never was (drawings preserved in the Casa Buonarotti, nos. 79 and 80; CB 94 is Michelangelo's drawing for the reading desks). A letter of April 3, 1526 indicates the Pope's desire to have the ceiling design reflect the division of the floor into three passages (the outer two later eliminated) and two rows of benches.

This selective review of the extraordinary documentation reveals that the idea of the library was at least five years old when construction began in the summer of 1524, that the design was from the beginning for an unvaulted hall, although until March 10, 1524 the Pope had hoped for an overhead vault but finally settled for vaults only beneath the library, that the present site was established by April 3, 1524, and that by August 2, 1524, with preliminary work begun, Michelangelo's design for a cruciform library had been dropped, and, except for a projected room at the end of the library that was never built, the definitive design in all but minor details was more or less in hand. The documentation reveals that there existed a unique collaboration between client and architect, and that the client must be credited with some aspects of the design, such as the general lines of the ceiling. The documentation also indicates that the placement of the library within the existing monastery was a matter of convenience to the entire complex, and not dictated by a preferred orientation. And finally, it suggests the overruling concern of the patron for the creation of the maximum protection from fire.

Bibliography (Selected): G. Milanesi, *Le lettere di Michelangelo Buonarotti*, Florence, 1875; A. Gotti, *Vita di Michelangelo Buonarotti*, Florence, 1875; K. Frey, *Sammlung ausgewählter Briefe an Michelangniolo Buonarotti*, Berlin, 1899, pp. 204 ff.; R. Wittkower, "Michelangelo's Biblioteca Laurenziana," *Art Bulletin*, XVI, 1934, pp. 123-218; C. de Tolnay, "La bibliothèque laurentienne de Michel-Ange," *Gazette des Beaux-Arts*, XIV, 1935, pp. 95-105; *idem*, "Un 'pensiero' nuovo di Michelangelo per il soffitto della libraria Laurenziana," *Critica d'Arte*, N.S. II, 1955, pp. 237 ff.; J. S. Ackerman, *The Architecture of Michelangelo*, London, I, 1961, pp. 33-34; II, pp. 33-42 (revised ed., Penguin Books, 1970, pp. 97-122, 313-317); G. Vasari, *La vita di Michelangelo*, ed. P. Barrochi, Milan, III, 1962, pp. 860 ff.; P. Portoghesi, "La biblioteca laurenziana," in *Michelangiolo architetto*, eds. P. Portoghesi and B. Zevi, Turin, 1964, pp. 209-350, 856-865; G. Corti, "Una ricordanza di Giovan Battista Figiovanni," *Paragone*, No. 175, 1964, pp. 24-31.

In addition to specifically architectural studies see E. Piccolomini, "Delle condizione e delle vicende della libreria medicea privata dal 1494 al 1508," *Archivio storico italiano*, 3d Ser., XIX, 1874, pp. 101-129, 254-281; XX, pp. 51-94; XXI, pp. 282 ff.; and P. D'Ancona and F. Baldasseroni, "La biblioteca della basilica fiorentina di San Lorenzo nei secoli XIV e XV," *Rivista delle biblioteche e degli archivi*, XVI, 1905, pp. 175-201.

23. *Florence, S. Marco.* Figs. 14A, 38-43.

The old Silvestrine monastery of S. Marco was given to the Dominican Observantists in a bull of Eugene IV dated January 21, 1436, and was occupied by friars from S. Domenico in Fiesole the following month. The existing buildings were in bad repair, but according to Lapaccini's Chronicle (Morçay), the friars lived in them for two years before rebuilding began under the patronage of Cosimo de'Medici and his brother, Lorenzo. Vespasiano da Bisticci and Antonino tell us that Cosimo undertook the rebuilding at the request of the Pope, but no contemporary document specifies the architect. The traditional attribution to Michelozzo is based upon Vasari's account, which has never been challenged.

Construction began in 1438 with the rebuilding of the old dormitory on the east side of the cloister of S. Antonino, and the tribune of the church was begun this same year. The latter was dedicated in 1443 but construction in the monastery continued into the 1460s. The date of the beginning of the library is undocumented, but Lapaccini tells us that it was finished by 1443. The first building did not last long, however, for it was knocked down by an earthquake in 1453 according to Biscioni, and not rebuilt until 1457, when the small room at the north end of the basilical space, the Greek Library, was added. Gori-Monta-nelli's interesting suggestion that the barrel vault above the central aisle was not built until this rebuilding is unfounded upon fact.

The room occupies the upper floor of the building forming the east wing of the cloister of S. Domenico, and running northward from the center of the dor-mitories surrounding the cloister of S. Antonino. It is a long, narrow space, 45.1 by 10.45 meters, divided into three aisles by two rows of 11 Ionic columns. The columns, bases, capitals, arches springing from column to column along the cen-tral passage, and the moulding running along the base of the central barrel vault, are all of *pietra serena,* which contrasts with the white stucco walls and vaults in typical Florentine fashion. The room was originally lighted by series of small windows centered in each bay on the side aisles. It has been restored since World War II.

Filarete describes the room thus:

della libreria non dico lagrandezza e labellezza dessa laquale e in uolta dalle colonne essa uolta e retta e diquello che debbia degnia uno libreria nonmanche cioe delibri.

Vasari followed Filarete's lead, but augmented his description by first-hand knowledge of the room:

Dopo [l'anno 1439], fu fatta la libreria, lunga braccia ottanta e large diciotto, tutta in volta di sopra e di sotto, e con sessantaquattro banchi di legno di cipresso, pieni di bellissimi libri.

The expression "vaulted above and below" means that the columns sustain brick vaults overhead, and rest upon the broad backs of the flat brick arches covering the rooms at ground level.

The 64 cypress desks mentioned by Vasari (whose account was followed by most later writers) were disposed in two equal rows, and held, among later additions, 400 volumes from the noted collection of the humanist Niccolò Niccoli, acquired by Cosimo for S. Marco when Niccolò died (1437) in debt.

Bibliography (Selected): R. Morçay, "La cronica del convento fiorentino di San Marco," *Archivio storico italiano,* LXXXI¹, 1913, pp. 1-29; Filarete, I, p. 321; II, fol 188r; Vespasiano pp. 10, 27-28, 441-442; S. Orlandi, *S. Antonino,* Florence, I, 1959-1960, pp. 179 ff.; II, pp. 57 ff.; Vasari, II, pp. 440-441; A. M. Biscioni, *Bibliothecae Mediceo-Laurentianae Catalogus,* Florence, 1852, pp. XV ff.; A. Visani, "La biblioteca del convento di San Marco in Firenze," *L'Archiginnasio,* XXXV, 1940, pp. 275-285; G. Marchini, "Il San Marco di Michelozzo," *Palladio,*

VI, 1942, 6, 113 n. 18; Morisani, pp. 46, 90-91; P. Redi, "Notizie storiche intorno al convento di S. Marco in Firenze," *Architetti* [Florence], IV, 1953, pp. 81-92; G. Morozzi, "Restauri nell'ex convento di S. Marco a Firenze," *Bolletino d'arte*, IV, 1955, pp. 350-354; L. Gori-Montanelli, *Brunelleschi e Michelozzo*, Florence, 1957, pp. 82 ff.; Cecchini, 1960, pp. 4-5; Cecchini, 1967, pp. 27-28.

24. **Florence, S. Maria del Carmine.*

The inventory of the books belonging to this Carmelite house indicates that some were kept in a special room. Mention is made in 1391 of the 113 volumes kept in the library on 14 reading desks (Humphreys translates *"scamno"* as shelf, but it is more likely that a reading desk is meant) probably arranged in one row. Paatz mentions unspecified work on the library as of 1464, but nothing else has yet come to light about this library.

Bibliography: Paatz, III, p. 189; K. W. Humphreys, *The Library of the Carmelites at Florence at the End of the Fourteenth Century*, Amsterdam, 1964.

25. *(Florence, S. Maria Novella.)*

The older of the two Dominican houses in Florence traces its origin to the founder himself. The church and monastery were erected in the late thirteenth and early fourteenth centuries. The provincial school of theology that existed here from the foundation was elevated to a *Studium Generale* in 1311.

In a later compilation of data from contemporary account books now lost is the following entry:

a. 1338. Si aggiusta una stanza, o altro luogo con colonne, e si appella in latino Armarius *per porvi i libri a catena per uso comune. a. 1340. Si fanno molte spese per la fabbrica* dell'Armario *per i libri del Comune. Di giugno si trova in quest'anno molte partite del fornaciaio* pro opere armarij. . . .

This library was enlarged in 1421 and later, and became a dormitory when a new library was erected between 1619 and 1636.

An inventory of the library in 1489 depicts a room with two rows of reading desks, the one of 22 desks *ex parte cimiterij*, the other of 24 desks *ex parte orti*. Six hundred and seven volumes are listed for this room (others are located *"in cassa que sub tabulis est"*). Padre Orlandi wrote me that this room was on the upper floor of the building north of the Chiostrino dei Morti (*cimiterij*) and overlooking the present Piazza della Stazione (where formerlly the *orti* were located). This room still exists but has been altered so many times that its original form could be determined only by archaeological investigation of the fabric. The "colonne" mentioned in the entry for 1338 quoted above are not in evidence now, and it is possible that the reference is to the columns beneath this room (Fig. 6, right). They predate the library itself. If columns were used and the room was arranged as a basilica, it would become the prime source for Michelozzo's room at S. Marco, the other Dominican house in Florence (Cat. 23). But given our present state of knowledge it is better to view the *dormitory* here (Figs. 6-7) as the type of space that suggested the form of the quattrocento library.

Bibliography: J. W. Brown, *The Dominican Church of Santa Maria Novella at Florence*, Edinburgh, 1902; Paatz, III, p. 670; S. Orlandi, *La biblioteca di S. Maria Novella in Firenze dal sec. XIV al sec. XIX*, Florence, 1952.

26. [*Florence, Convent of the Porta San Gallo.*]

The Austin Hermit monastery was rebuilt by Giuliano da Sangallo for Lorenzo de'Medici (Vasari). Poliziano mentions it as just finished in a letter of March 22, 1489; it was totally destroyed in the siege of Florence in 1530. What are probably plans of the church are in the Uffizi (Dis. arch. 1573, 1574). They show a church with unvaulted nave, but we know the monastery itself only from written sources. Richa published what he called a contemporary expense sheet for the various parts of the complex, but Fabriczy could not find his source in 1903. Richa's list includes the following: church 90 by 30 *braccia*, 31 *braccia* high, with 17 chapels [figures hard to reconcile with the Uffizi drawings] (cost: 3800 florins); square cloister 38 *braccia* on a side (2400 florins); refectory and library 45 by 18 *braccia*, 26 *braccia* high, "*in volta stimate*" (2500 florins); dormitory 127 by 20 *braccia*, 38 *braccia* high, with 37 cells, and two other dormitories "*a terrano*" (3800 florins); chapter room, *ospizio, foresteria,* and novitiate 48 by 18 by 28 *braccia* (3000 florins), second cloister 74 by 63 *braccia* (600 florins), two other cloisters, a kitchen, and "*volte sotterranee*" (300 florins), and a "*mura dell'orto*" 338 by 262 *braccia*, with chapel (600 florins).

Assuming Richa's source to have been reliable, and the schedule accurate, Giuliano's design cost Lorenzo only 1.4 florins per square *braccio* for the church (or nearly .05 florins per cubic *braccio*), whereas the building housing the refectory and library (the latter probably above the former) cost 3.1 florins per square *braccio* (or nearly .12 florins per cubic *braccio*). This difference in unit cost was probably due to the fact that the nave of the church was not vaulted (see the Uffizi drawings; Richa's schedule mentions no vaults in the church), while the dormitory and library building is described as vaulted by Richa's source. It is probably safe to assume that Lorenzo followed the design of Cosimo's library at S. Marco (Cat. 23); that is, that this vaulted room was a basilica.

We can get a vague impression of the appearance of the library from a letter to Eleonora, wife of Ercole I of Ferrara, from the court doctor Francesco Castelli, dated April 4, 1492. This mentions

Uno locho de una libreria amenissimo, lavorato se de arzento fusse hedificato cum una soscriptione sopra la porta facta in lectere maiuscule de farina marianesca: Sapientia hedificavit sibi locum.

Bibliography: Vasari, IV, p. 274; G. Richa, *Notizie istoriche delle chiese fiorentine,* Florence, I, 1754-1762, pp. 264 ff.; C. de Fabriczy, "Il convento di Porta San Gallo a Firenze," *L'Arte,* VI, 1903, pp. 381-384; G. Clausse, *Les San Gallo,* I, Paris, 1900-1902, pp. 120 ff.; G. Marchini, *Giuliano da Sangallo,* Florence, 1942, p. 89.

27. [*Florence, Sto. Spirito*]

The Florentine house of the Austin Hermits was founded in 1250, and became a *Studium Generale* of the Order in 1287. A series of recorded gifts and other notices traces the growth of the book collection through the fourteenth century. Inventories of 1450 and 1451 depict a library in two sections. The *Libraria maior* inventoried in 1450 contained 24 reading desks (in one row?) with an average of 16 volumes per desk. Vespasiano calls this the *"libreria de'frati."* Adjacent to this large room was a smaller one, the *libreria parva,* containing over a hundred volumes on eight reading desks. This smaller collection, described by Vespasiano as *"di là dalla libreria de' frati"* (beyond the friars' library), contained the books bequeathed by Boccaccio to the monastery (1387), and was inventoried in 1451. Vespasiano also tells us that Niccolò Niccoli (see Cat. 23) paid for the smaller library.

The monastery was rebuilt in the 1560s by Bartolomeo Ammannati and others, and the fifteenth-century library was replaced by a new room in 1564.

Bibliography: Vespasiano, pp. 27, 442; D. Gutiérrez, "La biblioteca di Santo Spirito in Firenze nella metà del secolo XV," *Analecta augustiana,* XXV, 1962, pp. 5-88; A. Mazza, "L' inventario della 'Parva Libraria' di Santo Spirito e la biblioteca del Boccaccio," *Italia medieovale e umanistica,* IX, 1966, pp. 1-74.

28. *Florence, Uffizi, Gabinetto dei Disegni, "Città ideale del Cav.re Giorgio Vasari."* Fig. 59.

Manuscript volume 28 by 39 cm., dated 1598, with a series of architectural designs in red, brown, and purple ink on white paper. By the historian's nephew.

A. Dis. arch. 4543r and 4544r contain, respectively, ground and upper floor plans of a monastery. The latter shows a library between cloisters, above the *foresteria,* and off the dormitory. The room is a long, narrow basilica with cross-vaulted side aisles; a barrel vault probably was intended above the central passage, which is narrower than side aisles. No windows indicated. Four *studietti* are located in corners of room.

B. Dis. arch. 4573r contains a plan of a public library in the form of a cruciform basilica with cross-vaulted side aisles, a barrel vault above the slightly narrower central aisle, and an octagonal cloister vault above the crossing. The room is entered from a lower *ricetto* by way of a stair with segmental steps. The "nave" was meant to contain Latin books, the "choir" Greek books, the "transepts" Hebrew and Vulgate works. Dis. arch. 4572v contains the following explanation:

Ancora in questo luogo giudicherei che fosse ben'fatto il farci una libreria publica, che ueramente è cosa nobile, e da tutte le parti lodeuole, se bene oggi ne pare, che sieno cosi necessarie, come anticamente p[er] hauersi facilmente più copia di libri p[er] cagione delle stampe, la doue gia ne si haueuano altri libri, che gli scritti à mano; Non di meno si renderebbe facile il diuenire sicomo grande à quelli, che nascessero di buono ingegno, e che dalle poche facoltà loro ne li è concesso il poter hauere gran copia di libri. Oltre che in simile *luoghi sono sempre tutti i libri, che molti particolari ancor che ricchi ne possa hauere. La presente pianta adunque potrebbe seruire, nella quale fra una colonna, e l'altra ho lasciato tanto di spatio, che ui si possono accomodare tre banchi, e diuiderei l'ordine de i libri come qui di sotto è contrasegnato.*

   A. Ricetto, ed entrata
   B. Luogo p[er] i libri Latini
   C. Luogo p[er] i libri Greci
   D. Luogo p[er] i libri hebraici
   E. Luogo p[er] i libri uulgari

The *ricetto* and *crociera* of the public library, and the *studietti* of the monastic layout, recall various features of Michelangelo's projects and executed designs for the Laurentian Library (Cat. 22). It is not impossible that Vasari could have had knowledge of unexecuted designs for the earlier library, and that consequently we have in these late basilical projects faint reflections of lost designs by Michelangelo himself.

Bibliography: W. von Oettingen, "Die sogenannte 'Idealstadt' des Ritters Vasari," *Repertorium für Kunstwissenschaft,* XIV, 1891, pp. 21 ff.; T. Zarebska, *Miasto idealne kawalera Giorgio Vasariego,* Warsaw, 1962.

29. *Forli, S. Giacomo (S. Biagio).
Reformed Dominican house visited in 1572 by Serafino Razzi who saw "una libreria di tre navi, in volta, con 19 banchi per lato."

Bibliography: Rotondi, p. 194; Kaeppeli, 1955, p. 6.

30. [Imola, S. Nicola].
Serafino Razzi saw this Dominican library in 1572:

La libreria è di xv banchi per lato, in capo di cui è un san Tommaso, con questo verso nella cattedra "Inter Doctores gloria prima Thomas."

No monastery of this name now exists in the city.

Bibliography: Rotondi, p. 195; Kaeppeli, 1955, pp. 6-7.

31. [Mantua, S. Agnese].
An inventory of 1427 of this Austin Hermit monastery locates the books in nine reading desks "versus lacum," and nine reading desks "versus ecclesiam." The library numbered 185 works. There is apparently no monastery of this name now in Mantua.

Bibliography: Gottlieb, p. 209.

32. [Mantua, S. Domenico].
An inventory of the collection here in 1417 lists 116 works without providing any architectural information. In 1572 Fra Serafino Razzi saw a library room having "16 banchi tutti nel mezzo, e poi d'intorno, intorno, due ordine di scaffali." This now appears to have been a rather unusual arrangement that might represent a transitional sixteenth-century combination of desks and shelves, although an inventory of 1449 of the library at S. Antonio in Padua (Cat. 40) suggests a similar arrangement there. Unfortunately the Mantuan house was pulled down with its church in 1924.

Bibliography: Rotondi, p. 211; Kaeppeli, 1955, p. 7; *Mantova domenicana*, Mantua, 1966, pp. 17-20.

33. [Mantua, S. Maria degli Angeli].
Serafino Razzi (1572) reported a library here with seven desks on each side. This Dominican monastery no longer exists.

Bibliography: Rotondi, p. 211; Kaeppeli, 1955, p. 7.

34. [*Milan, S. Ambrogio.*]

A project for a vaulted library is mentioned in 1497, probably by Bramante. The library never was executed.

Bibliography: P. Bondioli, *Il monastero di Sant'Ambrogio Maggiore di Milano,* Milan, 1935, pp. 31-32.

35. [*Milan, S. Eustorgio.*]

This Dominican monastery, the seat of an Inquisitional tribunal, became the *Studium Generale* of the Order in the fourteenth century.

A library is recorded as early as the end of the thirteenth century. An inventory of 1494 lists 722 volumes, 693 of which were stored in the library on 18 desks in two rows, one *"versus fontem,"* the other *"versus ortum."* This was the arrangement seen by Serafino Razzi when he visited the convent in 1572: "convento di due chiostri grandi e un piccolo; con libreria di nove banchi per lato." It was replaced in the 1680s.

Bibliography: Kaeppeli, 1955, pp. 5 ff.

36. [*Milan, S. Maria delle Grazie.*] Figs. 13D, 14D, 44-45.

In 1459 the Milanese asked the Vicar of the Congregation of S. Apollinare in Pavia to found a monastery of reformed Dominicans in their city. Ground was donated by Gaspero Vimercato, Captain-General of the Sforza troops, and the buildings erected under his patronage. The first stone was laid in August 1464, and the monastery *"pro maxima parte erectus"* by 1469. In the aerial bombardment of the city in 1943 the library erected as part of this new monastery was totally destroyed. Fortunately it had been previously published in detail in the series *Monumenti italiani.*

The book collection, which included over 127 works from the library of Pier Candido Decembrio left to the monastery by his widow in 1482, was stored in a basilical room which occupied the second floor of the wing, north of and parallel to the church, that separated the Chiostro dei Morti from the Chiostro Grande. This room was not centered upon the vaulted floor below. The south wall of the library rested upon the arcade of the Chiostro dei Morti while the north wall rose above the corresponding wall of the floor below. Between these two walls, the south row of columns rested upon the south wall of the lower story, but the north row had only the lower vaults to sustain it.

The room, 31 by 11.5 meters, was divided into three aisles by two rows of six Corinthian columns, and lighted through windows in every side bay. It was cross-vaulted throughout, although the vaults above the narrower central aisle were higher than those above the side aisles. The central series of bays, and their covering vaults, were smaller than those of the side aisles, and as a result, nine bays comprise the center, but only seven each side aisle. The resultant discrepancy in the layout of the vaults can be seen from the drawings. The possibility that Michelozzo, who is said to have been in Milan when the library was built, could have designed it is lessened when we compare the inept vaulting scheme here with his earlier accomplishment at S. Marco in Florence (Cat. 23).

When Serafino Razzi saw the library in 1572 there were 32 desks in each side aisle.

Bibliography: F. Malaguzzi-Valeri, *La corte di Ludovico il Moro*, II (*Bramante e Leonardo da Vinci*), Milan, 1915, pp. 8-9; Rotondi p. 204; A. Pica, *Il gruppo monumentale di S. Maria delle Grazie in Milano* (*I monumenti italiani*, 10), Rome, 1937; A. Pica and P. Portaluppi, *Le Grazie*, Rome, 1938; Kaeppeli, 1955, p. 7.

37. *Milan, S. Vittore al Corpo.* Figs. 13E, 14G, 46-48.

This Benedictine monastery was given to the Olivetans in 1507, and rebuilding began the following year. Older attributions to Alessio Tramello, who designed the similar layout at S. Sepolcro in Piacenza (Cat. 47), have been rejected by Gazzola. The first building campaign lasted only until 1525. Work was resumed in 1553 under the direction of Vincenzo Seregni. Whether the design of the library belongs to the earlier or later campaign (its actual construction probably belongs to the later) remains a matter of conjecture, but the monastery is all of a piece, and I believe planned as it is from the beginning. It was restored after partial destruction during World War II, and now forms part of the Museo Nazionale della Scienza e Tecnica Leonardo da Vinci. Nothing is known about the book collection here.

The library, 38.65 by 15.65 meters, occupies the top story of the two and one-half story wing separating two cloisters, south-east of and perpendicular to the church. It is centered upon lower supports.

The room is divided by two rows of nine Tuscan columns. The central aisle, wider than the side aisles, is covered by flat cross-vaults which spring from a point above the top of the lateral modified cross-vaults (similar to those at S. Sepolcro in Piacenza). The increased height of the central aisle permitted the builders to include a clerestory in the form of a series of oculi. There are other windows in every bay of the lower side walls. The rectangular "apse" at the north-west end of the room is not an original arrangement.

Bibliography: H. Hoffmann, "Die Entwicklung der Architektur Mailands von 1550-1650," *Wiener Jahrbuch für Kunstgeschichte*, IX, 1934, p. 68; P. Gazzola, "Alessio Tramello e il convento di S. Vittore in Milano," *Bollettino storico piacentino*, XXXII, 1937, pp. 10-13; C. Baroni, *L'Architettura lombarda da Bramante al Richini*, Milan, 1941, p. 123; F. Reggiori, *Il monastero olivetano di S. Vittore al Corpo in Milano,* Milan, 1954; G. Uccelli, "Danni di guerra e restauro dell'antico monastero di S. Vittore in Milano," *Atti del V convegno nazionale di storia dell' architettura,* 1948 [1957], pp. 613-621.

38. *Modena, S. Domenico.*

In 1572 Serafino Razzi saw a library here *"di 20 banchi per lato, ma con pochi libri."* This Dominican monastery remains in the city.

Bibliography: Rotondi, p. 196; Kaeppeli, 1955, p. 7.

39. *Monteoliveto Maggiore.* Figs. 13F, 14H, 49.

This was the Olivetan mother house, south-east of Siena, founded in 1313. The present library, erected between 1513 and 1516 (the date inscribed above the entrance), is the third one recorded here. The first, erected between 1447 and 1451, was furnished and stocked by provision of the will of Lodovico Petrucciani da Terni, a doctor of law at the Studio in Siena. We know nothing of the appearance of this room, or of its replacement that was built between 1497 and 1501. The present basilical room is traditionally attributed to Fra Giovanni da Verona, who carved the magnificent wooden doors at the entrance, but this attribution is not supported by documents.

The room, 25.9 by 9.9 meters, is located on the upper floor above the refectory in the west wing of the first cloister, lying to the south of the church. A section through this wing would reveal that the columns here rest upon the back of the broad vault above the refectory. This lower vault was rebuilt to take the additional load placed upon it when the library was added.

The library here is very similar to Michelozzo's at S. Marco in Florence (Cat. 23). The two rows of six Composite columns sustain cross-vaults above the side aisles and a barrel vault above the central passage. Unlike the earlier library, however, the side walls here are divided into bays by pilasters corresponding to the inner columns, and the room is illuminated by one window in every other bay of the west wall only.

Bibliography: L. Zdekauer, *Lo studio di Siena nel rinascimento*, Milan, 1894, pp. 89-90; L. Fratti, "I codici dell'abbazia di Monte Oliveto Maggiore presso Siena," *Bollettino della Società bibliografica italiana*, I, 1898, pp. 63-67; G. M. Thomas, *L'Abbaye de Monte-Olivet-Majeur*, Siena, 1898, pp. 181-182, 216; Cecchini, 1960, pp. 12-13; E. Carli, *L'Abbazia di Monteoliveto*, Milan, 1961; Cecchini, 1967, pp. 33-34.

40. [*Padua, S. Antonio.*]

An inventory of this Franciscan collection made in 1396-1397 lists 426 works in four groups: 114 items chained to 24 desks in two rows in the *armarium*, 33 items chained outside the library, 205 items unchained and outside the library, and 74 items on loan to friars in the monastery. By 1449 the collection had more than doubled, to 907 volumes, stored on a combination of desks (two rows of 14 each) and shelves (*scaffa;* 25 in two groups of 12 and 13 each). A similar arrangement could be found at S. Domenico in Mantua (Cat. 32) according to Serafino Razzi.

The interior of the present Biblioteca Antoniana stems from the eighteenth century.

Bibliography: K. W. Humphreys, *The Library of the Franciscans of the Convent of St. Antony, Padua at the Beginning of the Fifteenth Century*, Amsterdam, 1966.

41. **Padua, SS. Filippo e Giacomo (Chiesa degli Eremitani.)*
Michele Savonarola describes the library here as follows:

Alterum vero locum gloriosum primo in aspectu iucundissimum nimis nominabo, quem Bibliothecam Eremitanorum appellant, cuius ingressus librorum pulcritudine, eorumque multitudine homines in admirationem ducit. Locus enim amplissimus est, vitreis fenestris et lucidus et ornatus, cuius superiora scampna parte ad septentrionem versa: que grammatice, que rethorice, que loyce, que philosophie attinent, libros speciosos cum catenis tenent. Hacque in parte in mechanica plurimi et in theologia collocantur. Altera vero ad meridiem versa: que decretis, que decretalibus, que novo et veteri Testamento ettinent.

From this we get a picture of a windowed hall with two rows of reading desks. The *Libellus* was written in the 1440s.

Bibliography: M. Savonarole, *Libellus de Magnificis Ornamentis Regie Civitatis Padue*, A. Segarizzi, ed., Città di Castello, 1902, p. 56; Gutiérrez, 1954, pp. 240-251.

42. *Padua, S. Giovanni di Verdara*. Fig. 50.

This was the monastery of the white Benedictines founded in 1221. By 1423 the "community" had been reduced to one monk; a bull of Eugene IV of 1436 describes the buildings as ruins. In 1430 the monastery was joined to the reform-minded Regular Canons of the Lateran, and new buildings were begun in 1446, and the book collection began with a donation in 1443. Major gifts by Battista del Legname (1455) of 101 volumes, by Pietro da Montagnana (1478) of over 90 works, and especially by Giovanni Marcanova, a doctor of medicine at the local *studium* (1468), of 521 manuscripts, plus a constant stream of smaller donations, finally made the construction of a library necessary. The date of the building is unrecorded, but it must fall between Marcanova's gift and 1492, when Pietro Antonio degli Abati contracted for the desks. Cecchini is probably correct in assigning it to the early 1490s; he suggests Lorenzo da Bologna, documented for other work here, as builder and perhaps designer. The room has been altered for use as a hospital chapel.

The library is located on the upper floor between cloisters, south of and parallel to the former church. It is covered with one pointed vault which rises to a ridge high above the central axis of the space. The lower sides of this vault are broken by series of tall lunettes that seem to rest upon the pilasters dividing the side walls into bays. The upper zone of the side walls, which extends into the lunettes and is therefore above the spring of the vault, is perforated by circular windows let into every other bay. The lower zone is opened in alternate bays by round-arched windows. Since upper and lower openings are not in the same bays, but alternate from bay to bay, a complicated rhythm is set up between the windows themselves, and this is enriched by fresco tondi between the circular windows, and fresco panels between the lower windows:

b a b a b a b a b a b

A B A B A B A B A B A

The lower panels depict scholars at work in their studies.

Bibliography: G. M. U. de Gheltof, "La chiesa e convento di S. Giovanni di Verdara in Padova," *Bullettino di arti e curiosità veneziane*, IV, 1894, pp. 10-14; A. Barzan, *Affreschi scoperti nella biblioteca del monastero di S. Giovanni di Verdara*, Padua, 1946 (which I have not seen); P. *Atti dell'Istituto veneto*, 114, 1955-1956, plla biblioteca di S. Giovanni di Verdara in Padova," Sambin, "La formazione quattrocentesca dep. 263-271; *Padova, guida ai monumenti e alle opere d'arte*, Venice, 1961, pp. 420 ff.; Cecchini, 1967, pp. 35-37.

43. [*Padua, S. Giustina.*]

This was a Benedictine monastery, and the seat of the reformed Congregation of S. Giustina from 1409.

In 1461 *"per opera di Bernardo Terzi, detto il Piacentino, sorse un'ampia sala di biblioteca posta fra i due chiostri del Capitolo e delle Pitture."* The room now said to have been this library is at ground level, and looks more like a former refectory. The area above is inaccessible.

Bibliography: L. A. Ferrai, "La biblioteca di S. Giustina in Padova," in Giuseppe Mazzatinti, *Inventario dei manoscritti italiani delle biblioteche di Francia,* II, Rome, 1887, pp. 549-661.

44. *Parma, S. Giovanni Evangelista.* Figs. 13G, 14I, 51-52.

This was a Benedictine monastery founded in the tenth century, and joined the Congregation of S. Giustina in 1477. The present monastery was erected between 1490 and 1540. Although I have perused the index to the Benedictine Archive at the Archivio di Stato in Parma, and a *spoglia* of the monastery's account book from 1467 to 1588 in the Biblioteca Palatina in Parma, I have been unable to document the construction of the library itself. The guide to the monastery sold by the monks gives the date 1523, and this is reasonable on stylistic grounds.

The library is located on the upper floor of a building north of and perpendicular to the church. This building separates the older Chiostro del Capitolo (finished 1500) from the later Chiostro della Porta (1538). The structural members of the library are centered upon those of the floor below: the inner columns resting upon parallel walls at ground level, and the outer walls rising above the cloister arcades.

Within the library, the dimensions of which are 21.2 by 12.4 meters, the ten Ionic columns are arranged in two rows and placed upon pedestals. Each bay is covered with a cross-vault identical to all its neighbors, and all of these vaults spring from the tops of the columns. The aisles are therefore of equal width. The room is lighted by large windows in every other bay, and above each of these is another semicircular opening (original?). The decorative program is a later enrichment (1574-1576) by Giovanni Antonio Paganini and Ercole Pio.

Bibliography: A. I. Boselli, "Le pitture della biblioteca dell'ex-convento dei benedettini in Parma," *Aurea Parma,* II, 1913, pp. 167-172; L. Testi, "I corali miniati della chiesa di S. Giovanni

Evangelista in Parma," *La Bibliofilia,* XX, 1918-1919, pp. 1-30, 132-152; *San Giovanni Evangelista di Parma* (Guide), Parma, 1961; Cecchini, 1967, p. 34.

45. *Perugia, S. Domenico.* Figs. 14E, 53-54.

The friary was founded in the thirteenth century. By 1269 it housed a *Studium Artium* of the Dominican Provincia Romana; later philosophy and theology were added. By the fifteenth century it had reached the rank of *Studium Solemne* of theology, beneath the dignity of a *Studium Generale* (which for this province was in Florence). The friars joined the Observantist movement in 1437.

The book collection dates to the founding of the house. By 1309 it was in a room of its own, although a document of 1388 suggests that this or its replacement was no larger than an ordinary monk's cell. A series of inventories from 1430 on permit us to trace the continued growth of the collection through the fifteenth century, and to ascertain that part of it was stored on the nine reading desks in a *libraria maior* near the sacristy. In 1474 Leonardo Mansueti, elected Master General of the Order in that year, began the construction of a new room to house the existing collection plus his own library of nearly 500 volumes. A contract of 1481 calls for the fabrication of 18 desks for the library (certainly more were needed) which was in use in the following year. Unfortunately the inventory of the books ordered by the Comune in 1482 has not been found. The room was restored in the 1950s, but is still almost one full bay shorter than it was originally.

The library, originally 28 by 10.5 meters, is located on the upper floor of a brick structure that forms the south side of the older, or eastern cloister. The north elevation is broken at ground level by an irregular series of pointed arches, and above these are the traces of former windows. These could not have been the original windows for the library, because their sills fall below the present second-floor line. So this library resulted from a rebuilding of an earlier structure, probably part of the original fourteenth-century monastery. The internal columns of the library rest upon parallel walls at ground level, and the north wall at least (that to the south was inaccessible), rests upon the arcade mentioned above.

Seven Composite columns form each of the two rows that divide this library into three aisles of nearly equal width. All of the bays are identical in plan, so identical cross-vaults could be used throughout the room. Those above the central aisle, however, are raised higher than those over the lateral aisles. The room is illuminated through windows centered in every other bay.

Bibliography: G. Cecchini, "La quattrocentesca biblioteca del convento di S. Domenico di Perugia," *Miscellanea di scritti vari in memoria di Alfonso Gallo,* Florence, 1956, pp. 249-254;

Cecchini, 1960, pp. 10-11; T. Kaeppeli, *Inventari di libri di San Domenico di Perugia (1430-80)*, Rome, 1962; Cecchini, 1967, p. 31.

46. [*Piacenza, S. Giovanni in Canale.*]

When Serafino Razzi visited this Dominican house in 1572 he found a library *"con tre navi in volta, e tutta verde,"* which contained 31 desks in each lateral aisle. Conte Emilio Nasali-Rocca has informed me by letter that this library no longer exists.

Bibliography: Rotondi, p. 196; Kaeppeli, 1955, p. 8.

47. *Piacenza, S. Sepolcro.* Figs. 13C, 14F, 55-57.

This Olivetan monastery was formed in 1484. Reconstruction began in 1488 from the design of Alessio Tramello. Documents published by Roi date the library construction to 1508 or 1509. Nothing is known about the collection here. The monastery now forms part of the Ospedale civile.

Tramello's monastic buildings lie to the south of the church. They are organized around two major cloisters divided by a building nearly parallel to the church. This contains the library on its upper floor. A transverse section through this wing reveals a continuous, symmetrical structural system with the inner columns of the library above resting upon parallel walls at ground level, and the outer walls resting upon the cloister arcades. The building is covered with a low gable resting directly upon the library vaults. Traces of fresco on the south exterior wall suggest that the exterior was once covered with bright designs, but their present condition makes it impossible to be certain of their date.

The library, 37.1 by 11.7 meters, is divided into three aisles of equal width by two rows of nine rather thin columns with crude Corinthian capitals. The columns cannot be blamed on Tramello, because one of the documents published by Roi tells us that *"Magistro donato [scarpellino] . . . non ha dato le colone dl libraria d la longeza ut grosetia secondo ch haueua promessa . . ."* The central passage is covered by a series of pointed cross-vaults, whereas the side aisles are topped with cross-vaults that meet the side walls in two lunettes per bay. A continuous severy running from end to end of the side aisles draws all the bays into a unit. There is one window in the center of each bay.

Bibliography: P. Roi, "La chiesa e il convento di S. Sepolcro in Piacenza," *Bollettino d'arte*, 2d ser., III, 1923-1924, pp. 356-379; P. Gazzola, *Opere di Alessio Tramello (I monumenti italiani, 5)*, Rome, 1935; G. Cecchini, 1967, pp. 31-32.

48. [*Rimini, S. Francesco.*]

Sigismondo Malatesta included a library in his rebuilding of this monastery after 1450. We know nothing about it, but Ricci believed it to have been of little architectural interest.

In 1475 Roberto Valturio left his library to this monastery on the condition that the collection by moved to an upper floor. All that is left of his library is a plaque recording the date of the move in 1490. An inventory of the library of 1560 published by Mazzatinti lists a collection of some 300 volumes stored in 40 reading desks divided into two equal rows.

Bibliography: G. Mazzatini, "La biblioteca di san Francesco (Tempio Malatestiano) in Rimini," *Scritti vari di filologia dedicati a Ernesto Monaci,* Rome, 1901, pp. 345-352; Corrado Ricci, *Il Tempio malatestiano,* Milan and Rome [1924], pp. 226 ff.; D. Fava, "Fra Giovanni Ferrarese e Sigismondo Pandolfo Malatesta," *Scritti vari dedicati a Mario Armanni,* Milan, 1938, pp. 49-62.

49. **Rome, S. Agostino.*

This is an Austin Hermit monastery founded in 1287. The fifteenth-century monastery was rebuilt by Vanvitelli in 1747.

An inventory of the books, dated 1432, provides no information of architectural significance. A second inventory, of 1478, lists 413 books on 16 reading desks, all but two of which are divided into a *"primo"* and a *"secundo latere."*

Bibliography: D. Gutiérrez, "La biblioteca di Sant'Agostino di Roma nel secolo XV," *Analecta augustiniana,* XXXVII, 1964, pp. 5-58; XXVIII, 1965, pp. 57-153.

50. **Rome, S. Marcello.*

From a 1406 inventory of the library of this Servite house we learn that a small collection of 67 items was stored on five reading desks, one *"versus plateam,"* two *"versus sacristiam"* (each at a window), one *"versus ecclesiam et ortum"* (also near a window), and one *"versus plateam, sacristiam et ecclesiam."* This seems a rather haphazard arrangement.

Bibliography: R. Taucci, "Delle biblioteche antiche dell'ordine e dei loro cataloghi," *Studi storici sull'Ordine dei Servi di Maria,* II, 1935-1936, pp. 158-168, 215-216.

51. **Siena, S. Francesco.*

An inventory of 1481 (Siena, Biblioteca Comunale, C. IV 19, fols. 91-205: a seventeenth-century copy) indicates books chained to benches divided into two rows. Those benches to the left are described as new. There are 16 of them containing 218 volumes. The benches to the right are not described as new, and differ in design from those on the left. The right (older?) row begins and ends with a one-sided bench placed against the (end) wall of the room; in between there are ten other benches (for a total of 12), each with two faces. This row contains 273 volumes; the library as a whole contained 499 volumes including eight listed as unchained and unlocated. There were fewer benches in the right row because double-faced benches would require more room than single-faced ones.

The seventeenth-century manuscript from which the above information was taken goes on to list a total of 1336 works, the remainder stored in ambries. These represent later additions to this library.

This inventory has been mentioned several times, but never accurately described. Hefele followed Zdekauer in reporting more than 1300 volumes and locating the library in the Osservanza outside the city. It is more likely that this inventory should be connected with the Franciscan house within the city. Clark misread the number of volumes chained to reading desks.

Bibliography: Gottlieb, p. 245; L. Zdekauer, *Lo studio di Siena,* Milan, 1894, pp. 91-92; Clark, p. 201; K. Hefele, *Der hl. Bernardin von Siena,* Freiburg i. B., 1912, p. 14.

52. [*Venice, S. Giorgio Maggiore.*] Fig. 58.

This was a Benedictine house that joined the Congregation of S. Giustina in 1418; separated in 1430; rejoined in 1443. Since the rebuilding of the monastery in the late sixteenth and seventeenth centuries under Palladio and Longhena, the library, said by Vasari to have been erected by Cosimo de'Medici from a design by Michelozzo in 1433, has disappeared, almost without a trace. The earliest mention of Cosimo's gift of a library to S. Giorgio that has come to my attention is a passage in Albertini (1515).

Olmo, the seventeenth-century chronicler of the monastery, rejected Vasari's account, and basing his attribution upon an inscription he found in the library, gave the design to Giovanni Lanfredini, who, he said, erected the building between 1464 and 1478. Cicogna in turn rejected Olmo's opinion on the basis of a document he said was undated but certainly of about 1478. This document mentioned the "old library." The monastery did possess a collection of books before Cosimo's gift, but we have no record of a building to house it, so Cicogna's document must refer to Michelozzo's library. Recent criticism has reconciled these conflicting opinions by assigning the beginning of the library to Michelozzo (who was in Venice for only a year apparently), and the completion or extension to Lanfredini.

Four documents tell us something about the building. The view of the complex in the panoramic map of Venice of about 1500 by Jacopo de'Barbari shows a long, two-story block with gable roof standing perpendicularly to the church. This might have been the library. Two tall Gothic *bifore* like those Michelozzo used at this time at SS. Annunziata in Florence (Cat. 19) punctuate the end of this block. The second source is a plan project for church and monastery attributed to Tullio Lombardo and dated 1520 or 1521 by Timofiewitsch. This shows the area beneath the library and between the two cloisters. If we could be certain that the room occupied the whole upper floor of this wing, we would have some idea of its proportions. Finally, Olmo gives a very brief description of the room:

Aveva questa fabbrica il tetto toccato ad oro con vaghe e non volgari pitture, ed erano le pareti coperte di tavole pure dipinte. . . .

And Vasari himself tells us that it

fu finita non solo di muraglia, di banchi, di legnami ed altri ornamenti, ma repiena di molti libri.

From the evidence we have I believe it is possible to reconstruct this library as a hall with gilded ceiling (of unknown date) and walls covered with paintings (also undated). It was probably lighted from the sides and ends by tall *bifore* as at SS. Annunziata, which indeed it probably resembled very closely.

Bibliography: F. Albertini, *Opusculus mirabilibus noue e ueteris Urbis Rome* . . . , Rome, 1515, f. 90v; Vasari, II, p. 434; A. M. Biscioni, *Bibliothecae Mediceo-Laurentianae Catalogus*, Florence, 1752, pp. XII-XIV; E. A. Cicogna, *Delle inscrizioni veneziane*, IV, 1834, pp. 594 ff.; Morisani, p. 89; G. Damerini, *L'isola e il cenobio di San Giorgio Maggiore*, Venice, 1956, pp. 51 ff.; W. Timofiewitsch, "Ein neuer Beitrag zu der Baugeschichte von S. Giorgio Maggiore," *Bolletino del centro internazionale di studi di architettura Andrea Palladio*, V, 1963, pp. 330-339.

53. **Verona, S. Zeno Maggiore.*

The act giving this house to the Benedictines of Subiaco (1425) lists a cloister, chapter room, large refectory, old dormitory *"ubi nunc horem, seu granaria, cum loco pro Libraria,"* and a cellar *"cum Curticella, et Furno, et loco subtus Li-*

brariam." In 1400 the monastery had 131 works, all kept in the sacristy, so this library must have been erected in the first quarter of the century. Its elevated position is typical, but not its obscure and precarious location near the granary and ovens.

Bibliography: M. Carrara, "La biblioteca del monastero di S. Zeno Maggiore di Verona," *Rivista di storia della chiesa in Italia,* VI, 1952, pp. 411-426.

54. [*Vicenza, S. Corona.*] Fig. 60.

The collection of books in this Dominican monastery goes back to the thirteenth century, but little is known about its history. The library was constructed with funds left by Cristoforo Barbarano in 1496. All but the western wall, apparently, was destroyed during an aerial bombardment of the city in 1944.

Available photographs show the library to have been a basilical space divided by rows of six Composite columns set upon pedestals. The side aisles were certainly covered with cross-vaults, but at this writing the vault above the central aisle is in doubt. The room was illuminated by rather large rectangular windows in each bay, and originally frescoed with portraits of famous Dominican scholars.

Bibliography: D. Bortolan, *S. Corona,* Vicenza, 1889, pp. 61 ff.; E. Arslan, *Vicenza (Catalogo delle cose d'arte . . . d'Italia),* Rome, I, 1956, p. 71; F. Barbieri, R. Cevese, L. Magagnato, *Guida di Vicenza,* Vicenza, 2d ed., 1956, p. 153; G. Mantese, *Memorie storiche della chiesa vicentina,* Vicenza, III², 1964, pp. 861, 964.

Bibliography

Works listed in the Catalogue are not repeated here unless they are of general content.

The bibliography is divided into the following parts. The numbering is continuous throughout, although the works are arranged alphabetically in each part.

A. The Medieval University and the Monastic School

B. Observantism

C. Library History, General

D. Library History, Italy

E. Library Architecture, General

F. Library Architecture, Italy

G. Miscellaneous

A.

1. C. F. Bühler, *The University and the Press in Fifteenth-Century Bologna*, Notre Dame, 1958.

2. F. Cavazza, *Le scuole dell'antico studio bolognese*, Milan, 1896.

3. L. J. Daly, *The Medieval University 1200-1400*, New York, 1961.

4. H. S. Denifle, *Die Entstehung der Universitäten des Mittelalters*, Berlin, 1885.

5. C. Douais, *Essai sur l'organisation des études dans l'ordre des Frères Prêcheurs au treizième et au quatorzième siècle (1216-1342)*, Paris-Toulouse, 1884.

6. F. Ehrle, *I Più antichi statuti della facoltà teologica dell'università di Bologna*, Bologna, 1932.

7. G. Ermini, *Storia della università di Perugia*, Bologna, 1947.

8. H. Felder, *Geschichte der wissenschaftlichen Studien im Franziskanerorden bis um die Mitte des 13 Jahrhunderts*, Freiburg im B., 1904.

9. H. M. Féret, "Vie intellectuelle et vie scolaire dans l'ordre des Frères Prêcheurs," *Archives d'histoire dominicaine*, I, 1946, pp. 1-37.

10. R. Gherardi, *Statuti della università e studio fiorentino,* Florence, 1881.

11. P. Kibre, *The Nations in the Mediaeval Universities,* Cambridge, Mass., 1948.

12. J. Leclercq, *The Love of Learning and the Desire for God,* New York, 1961.

13. L. Maître, *Les écoles épiscopales et monastiques en Occident avant le universités,* Ligugé and Paris, 2d ed., 1924.

14. C. Malagota, *Statuti dell università a dei collegi dello studio bolognese,* Bologna, 1888.

15. G. Manacordà, *Storia della scuola in Italia,* Milan [1913].

16. B. M. Marti, *The Spanish College at Bologna in the Fourteenth Century,* Philadelphia, 1966.

17. C. Piana, *Ricerche su le università de Bologna e di Parma nel secolo XV,* Quaracchi, 1963.

18. H. Rashdall, *The Universities of Europe in the Middle Ages,* eds. F. M. Powicke and A. B. Emden, London, 1936.

19. N. Schachner, *The Mediaeval Universities,* New York, 1962.

20. A. Sorbelli, *Storia della università di Bologna,* Bologna, 1944-1947.

21. C. H. Talbot, "The Universities and the Mediaeval Library," *The English Library Before 1700,* eds. Francis Wormald and C. E. Wright, London, 1958, pp. 66 ff.

22. A. Visconti, *La storia dell'università di Ferrara (1391-1950),* Bologna, 1950.

23. G. Zaccagnini, "Le scuole e la libreria del convento di S. Domenico in Bologna," *Atti e memorie della R. Deputazioni di storia patria per la provincia di Romagna,* Ser. IV, XVII, 1927, pp. 228-327.

24. G. Zaccagnini, *Storia dello studio di Bologna durante il rinascimento,* Geneva, 1930.

25. G. Zaccagnini, *La vita dei maestri e degli scolari nello studio di Bologna nei secoli XIII e XIV,* Geneva, 1926.

B.

26. G. G. Coulton, *The Last Days of Medieval Monasticism (Five Centuries of Religion,* IV), Cambridge, 1950.

27. A. Dini-Traversari, *Ambrogio Traversari e i suoi tempi,* Florence, 1912.

28. M. Heimbucher, *Die Orden und Kongregationen der katholischen Kirche,* Paderborn, 1933-1934.

29. R. M. Huber, *A Documented History of the Franciscan Order,* Washington, D. C., 1944.

30. T. Leccisotti, "La congregazione benedettina di S. Giustina e la riforma della chiesa al secolo XV," *Archivio della reale deputazione romana di storia patria,* LXVII, 1944, pp. 451-469.

31. T. Leccisotti, "Per la storia della Congregazione Cassinese: tentativi di unione nei secoli XV-XVI," *Benedictina,* 10, 1956, pp. 61-74.

32. I. da Milano, "San Bernardino da Siena e l'Osservanza minoritica," *S. Bernardino. Saggi e ricerche pubblicati nel quinto centenario della morte (1444-1944),* Milan, 1944, pp. 379-406.

33. J. Moorman, *A History of the Franciscan Order,* Oxford, 1968.

34. L. Oliger "S. Bernardino e l'introduzione dell'Osservanza a Piacenza," *Bullettino di studi bernardiniani,* II, 1936, pp. 265-280.

35. *Ordini e congregazioni religiose,* ed. M. Escobar, Turin, 1951-1953.

36. I. Origo, *The World of San Bernardino,* New York, 1962.

37. S. Orlandi, *Il beato Lorenzo da Ripafratta,* Florence, 1956.

38. G. Penco, *Storia del monachesimo in Italia,* Rome, 1961.

39. P. Sambin, "Sulla riforma dell'ordine benedettino promossa da S. Giustina di Padova," in his *Ricerche di storia monastica medioevale,* Padua, 1959, pp. 69-122.
40. I. Tassi, "La crisi della Congregazione di S. Giustina tra il 1419 e il 1431," *Benedictina,* V, 1951, pp. 95-111.
41. I. Tassi, *Ludovico Barbo (1381-1443),* Rome, 1952.
42. B. Trifone, "Ludovico Barbo e i primordi della Congregazione benedettina di Santa Giustina," *Rivista storica benedettina,* V, 1910, pp. 269-280, 364-394; VI, 1911, pp. 366-392.
43. N. Widloecher, *La congregazione dei Canonici regolari lateranensi,* Gubbio, 1929.

C.

44. G. H. Becker, *Catalogi bibliothecarum antiqui,* Bonn, 1885.
45. G. A. E. Bogeng, *Die grossen Bibliophilen,* Leipzig, 1922.
46. C. F. Bühler, *The Fifteenth Century Book,* Philadelphia, 1960.
47. H. J. Chaytor, *From Script to Print,* New York, 1967.
48. L. DeLisle, *Le cabinet des manuscrits de la Bibliothèque Impériale [after Vol. I . . . Bibliothèque Nationale],* Paris, 1868-1881.
49. *Geschichte der Bibliotheken (Handbuch der Bibliothekwissenschaft,* III), ed. Georg Leyh, Wiesbaden, 1955-1957.
50. T. Gottlieb, *Ueber mittelalterliche Bibliotheken,* Leipzig, 1890 (reissued Graz, 1955).
51. D. Gutiérrez, "De antiquis ordinis eremitarum sancti augustini bibliothecis," *Analecta augustiniana,* XXIII, 1954, pp. 164-372.
52. A. Hessel, *Geschichte der Bibliotheken,* Göttingen, 1925.
53. R. Hirsch, *Printing, Selling and Reading, 1450-1550,* Wiesbaden, 1967.
54. K. W. Humphreys, *The Book Provisions of the Mediaeval Friars 1215-1400,* Amsterdam, 1964.
55. L. Jacob, *Traicté des plus belles bibliothèques publiques et particulieres,* Paris, 1644.
56. E. D. Johnson, *A History of Libraries in the Western World,* New York and London, 1965.
57. J. Lipsius, *De Bibliothecis Syntagma,* Antwerp, 1602 (English translation as Vol. V of *Literature of Libraries in the Seventeenth and Eighteenth Centuries,* eds. J. C. Dana and H. W. Kent, Chicago, 1907).
58. [J. Lomeier] *A Seventeenth-Century View of European Libraries. Lomeier's De Bibliothecis, Chapter X,* ed. and tr. J. W. Montgomery, Berkeley and Los Angeles, 1962.
59. G. H. Putnam, *Books and Their Makers During the Middle Ages,* New York, 1962 [reprint of 1896-1897 ed.].
60. K. Schottenloher, *Bücher bewegten die Welt,* Stuttgart, 1951-1952.
61. K. M. Setton, "From Medieval to Modern Library," *Proceedings of the American Philosophical Society,* 104, 1960, pp. 371-390.
62. J. W. Thompson, *The Medieval Library,* Chicago, 1939 (reissued New York, 1965).
63. O. Thyregod, *Die Kulturfunktion der Bibliothek,* The Hague, 1936.
64. B. L. Ullman, "The Sorbonne Library and the Italian Renaissance," in his *Studies in the Italian Renaissance,* Rome, 1955, pp. 41-53.
65 J. Vorstius, *Grundzüge der Bibliothek-Geschichte,* Leipzig, 1935.
66. W. Wattenbach, *Das Schriftwesen im Mittelalter,* Graz, 4th ed., 1958.

67. F. Wormald, "The Monastic Library," *The English Library Before 1700*, eds. F. Wormald and C. E. Wright, London, 1958, pp. 16 ff.

D.

68. G. Avanzi, *Libri, librerie, biblioteche nell'umanesimo e nella rinascenza*, Rome, 1954-1956.
69. G. Brugnoli, "La biblioteca dell'abbazia di Farfa," *Benedictina*, V, 1951, pp. 3-17.
70. F. Cognasso, *L'Italia nel rinascimento*, Turin, I, 1965, pp. 438-455.
71. P. Egidi, "L'Abazia di S. Martino al Cimino presso Viterbo," *Rivista storica benedettina*, II, 1907, pp. 481-552.
72. M. Esposito, "The Ancient Bobbio Catalogue," *Journal of Theological Studies*, XXXII, 1931, pp. 337-344.
73. F. Fiocco, "La biblioteca di Palla Strozzi," *Studi di bibliografia e di storia in onore di Tammaro de Marinis*, Verona, II, 1964, pp. 289-310.
74. A. Gallo, "Biblioteche abruzzesi e molisane," *Accademie e biblioteche d'Italia*, IV, 1930, pp. 126-143.
75. I. Giorgi, "L'Antica biblioteca di Nonantola," *Rivista delle biblioteche e degli archivi*, VI, 1895, pp. 54-60.
76. *Guida storica e bibliografica degli archivi e delle biblioteche d'Italia*, Rome, 1932-1940.
77. K. W. Humphreys, *The Library of the Carmelites at Florence at the End of the Fourteenth Century*, Amsterdam, 1964.
78. K. W. Humphreys, *The Library of the Franciscans of the Convent of St. Antony, Padua at the Beginning of the Fifteenth Century*, Amsterdam, 1966.
79. T. Kaeppeli, "La bibliothèque de Saint-Eustorge à Milan à la fin du XVe siècle," *Archivum fratrum praedicatorum*, XXV, 1955, pp. 5-74.
80. P. Kibre, "The Intellectual Interests Reflected in Libraries of the Fourteenth and Fifteenth Centuries," *Journal of the History of Ideas*, VII, 1946, pp. 257-297.
81. M.-H. Laurent, *Fabio Vigili et les bibliothèques de Bologne au début du XVIe siècle*, Vatican City, 1943.
82. G. Mazzatinti, *Inventario dei manoscritti delle biblioteche d'Italia*, Forli, 1890 ff.
83. G. Mercati, "Il catalogo della biblioteca di Pomposa," *Studi e documenti di storia e diritto*, XVII, 1896, pp. 143-177 (reprinted *idem, Opere minori*, Vatican City, I, 1937, pp. 358-388).
84. R. Sabbadini, *Le scoperte dei codici latini e greci ne' secoli XIV e XV*, Florence, 1905-1914 (reissued Florence, 1967).
85. L. Sighinolfi, "La biblioteca di Giovanni Marcanova," *Collectanea variae doctrinae Leoni S. Olschki*, Munich, 1921, pp. 187-222.
86. A. Sorbelli, *La biblioteca capitolare della cattedrale di Bologna nel secolo XV*, Bologna, 1904.
87. R. Taucci, "Delle biblioteche antiche dell'ordine e dei loro cataloghi," *Studi storici sull'Ordine dei Servi di Maria*, II, 1935-1936, pp. 145 ff.
88. *Tesori delle biblioteche d'Italia*, ed. D. Fava, Milan, 1932.

E.

88a. M. Brawne, *Libraries,* New York, 1970.

89. J. W. Clark, *The Care of Books,* Cambridge, 2d ed., 1909.

90. E. Lehmann, *Die Bibliotheksräume der deutschen Klöster im Mittelalter,* Berlin, 1957.

91. G. Leyh, "Das Haus und seine Einrichtung," *Handbuch der Bibliothekswissenschaft,* ed. F. Milkau, Leipzig, II, 1933, pp. 1-115.

92. J. Müller, "Bibliothek," *Reallexicon der deutschen Kunstgeschichte,* II, 1937, cols. 518-542.

93. N. Pevsner, "Libraries: Nutrimentum Spiritus," *Architectural Review,* CXXX, October 1961, pp. 240-244.

94. W. Schürmeyer, *Bibliotheksräume aus fünf Jahrhunderten,* Frankfurt a. M., 1929 (see review by Georg Leyh in *Zentralblatt für Bibliothekswesen,* 46, 1929, pp. 506-512).

95. B. H. Streeter, *The Chained Library,* London, 1931.

F.

96. E. Apolloni, *Cento biblioteche italiane,* Rome, 1964.

97. G. Cecchini, "Evoluzione archittonico-strutturale della biblioteca pubblica in Italia dal secolo XV al XVII," *Accademie e biblioteche d'Italia,* XXXV, 1967, pp. 27-47.

98. G. Cecchini, *6 biblioteche monastiche rinascimentali,* Milan, 1960.

99. W. Lotz, "The Roman Legacy in Sansovino's Venetian Buildings," *Journal of the Society of Architectural Historians,* XXII, 1963, pp. 3-12.

G.

100. J. S. Ackerman, *The Cortile del Belvedere,* Vatican City, 1954.

101. F. Antal, *Florentine Painting and its Social Background,* London, 1947.

102. M. Aubert, *L'Architecture cistercienne en France,* Paris, 2d ed., 1947.

103. M. Bottaglini, "La soppressione dei conventi nella repubblica romana giacobina," *Palatino,* IX, 1965, pp. 13-23.

104. C. Calzolai, *La storia della Badia a Settimo,* Florence, 1958.

105. F. L. Del Migliore, *Firenze; città nobilissima, illustrata,* Florence, 1684.

106. L. F. De Longhi, *L'Architettura delle chiese cistercensi italiane,* Milan, 1958.

107. C. Enlart, *Origines françaises de l'architecture gothique en Italie,* Paris, 1894.

108. *Filarete's Treatise on Architecture,* tr. J. R. Spencer, New Haven and London, 1965.

109. D. Fontana, *Della trasportatione dell'obelisco vaticano et delle fabriche di nostro signore Papa Sisto V,* Rome, 1590.

110. M. P. Gilmore, *The World of Humanism,* New York, 1952.

111. E. H. Gombrich, "The Early Medici as Patrons of Art," *Italian Renaissance Studies,* ed. E. F. Jacob, London, 1960, pp. 279-311.

112. L. Gori-Montanelli, *Brunelleschi e Michelozzo*, Fiorence, 1957.

113. C. H. Haskins, *The Renaissance of the Twelfth Century*, Cambridge, Mass., 1927.

114. L. H. Heydenreich, "Gedanken über Michelozzo di Bartolomeo," *Festschrift Wilhelm Pinder*, Leipzig, 1938, pp. 264-290.

115. P. La Cute, "Le vicende delle biblioteche monastiche veneziane dopo la soppressione napoleonica," *Venezia, rivista mensile della città*, VII, 1929, pp. 597 ff.

116. M. Meiss, *Painting in Florence and Siena After the Black Death*, New York, 1964.

117. O. Morisani, *Michelozzo architetto*, Milan, 1951.

118. S. Orlandi, *Necrologio di S. Maria Novella*, Florence, 1955.

119. W. Paatz, "Zur Baugeschichte des Palazzo de Podestà (Bargello) in Florenz," *Mitteilungen des kunsthistorischen Institutes in Florenz*, III, 1919-1932, pp. 287-321.

120. W. Paatz, *Werden und Wesen der Trecento-Architektur in Toskana*, Burg b. M., 1937.

121. W. and E. Paatz, *Die Kirchen von Florenz*, Frankfurt a. M., 1940-1954.

122. R. Papini, "Interpretazione di Antonello," *La Rinascita*, III, 1940, pp. 470-494.

123. L. Pastor, *The History of the Popes*, London, 1938-1950.

124. G. Richa. *Notizie istoriche delle chiese fiorentine*, Florence, 1754-1762.

125. G. Rotondi, "Fra Serafino Razzi e il suo viaggio in Lombardia nel 1572," *Archivio storico lombardo*, Ser. 6, LI, 1924, pp. 186-214.

126. F. Sansovino, *Venetia città nobilissima*, Venice, 1581.

127. C. M. von Stegmann and H. von Geymüller, *Die Architektur der Renaissance in Toscana*, Munich, 1885-1908.

128. A. della Torre, *Storia dell'accademia platonica di Firenze*, Florence, 1902.

129. G. Uzielli, *La vita e i tempi di Paolo dal Pozzo Toscanelli*, Rome, 1894.

130. G. Vasari, *Le vite de' più eccellenti pittori*, . . . , ed. G. Milanesi, Florence, 1878-1885 (reissued 1906).

131. V. da Bisticci, *Vite di uomini illustri del secolo XV*, eds. P. D'Ancona and E. Aeschlimann, Milan, 1951.

132. M. Wackernagel, *Der Lebensraum des Künstlers in der florentinischen Renaissance*, Leipzig, 1938.

133. E. H. Wilkins, *Life of Petrarch*, Chicago, 1961.

134. H. Willich, *Die Bankunst der Renaissance in Italien*, Berlin-Neubabelsberg, 1914.

135. G. Zippel, *Niccolò Niccoli*, Florence, 1890.

Illustrations

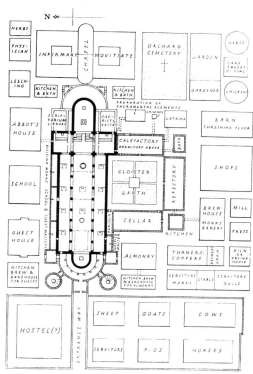

1. Plan for a monastery, ca. 820 (Chapter Library, St. Gall) (after K. Conant, *Carolingian and Romanesque Architecture,* Baltimore: Penguin, 1959)

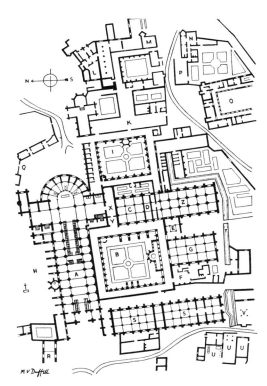

3. Clairvaux, Cistercian Abbey, twelfth century. Plan by Viollet-le-Duc (after *Encyclopaedia Britannica,* 1929).

2. Fossanova, Cistercian Abbey, twelfth century. Detail of plan showing cloister ambry and book room (after J. W. Clark, *The Care of Books,* Cambridge: University Press, 2d ed., 1909).

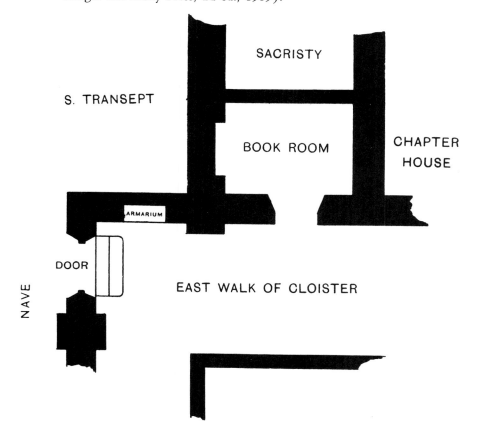

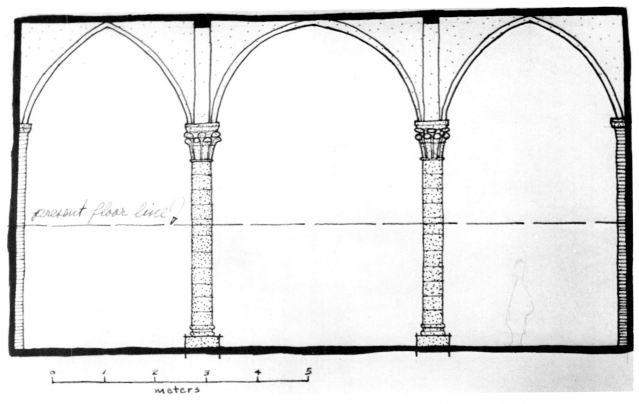

present floor line

meters

4. Badia a Settimo, Cistercian Abbey of S. Salvatore, thirteenth century. Section through so-called Pilgrim's Hall (author).

5. Badia a Settimo, Pilgrim's Hall, interior (photo: Alinari).

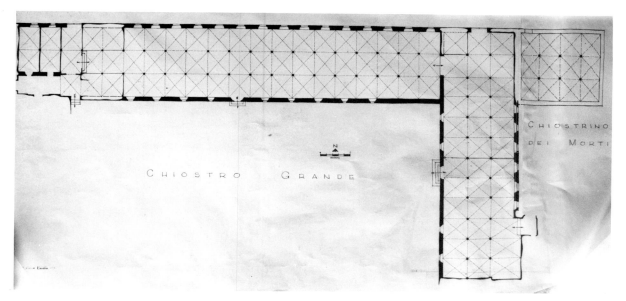

6. Florence, S. Maria Novella. Plan of north and east wings of the Chiostro Grande, thirteenth century (author).

7. Florence, S. Maria Novella. North wing of Chiostro Grande, interior (photo: Jean Baer O'Gorman).

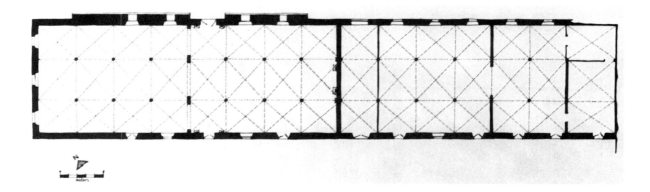

8. Florence, S. Domenico al Maglio. Plan of ground floor of thirteenth-century wing (author).

9. Florence, S. Domenico al Maglio. Thirteenth-century wing, interior (photo: Jean Baer O'Gorman).

10. Florence, S. Domenico al Maglio. Thirteenth-century wing, exterior (photo: Jean Baer O'Gorman).

11. Lorenzo Monaco, *St. Jerome in His Study,* *ca.* 1420 (Amsterdam, Rijksmuseum).

12. Sassetta, *St. Thomas Inspired By The Holy Ghost,* 1423-26 (Budapest, Szépmüvézeti Muzeum).

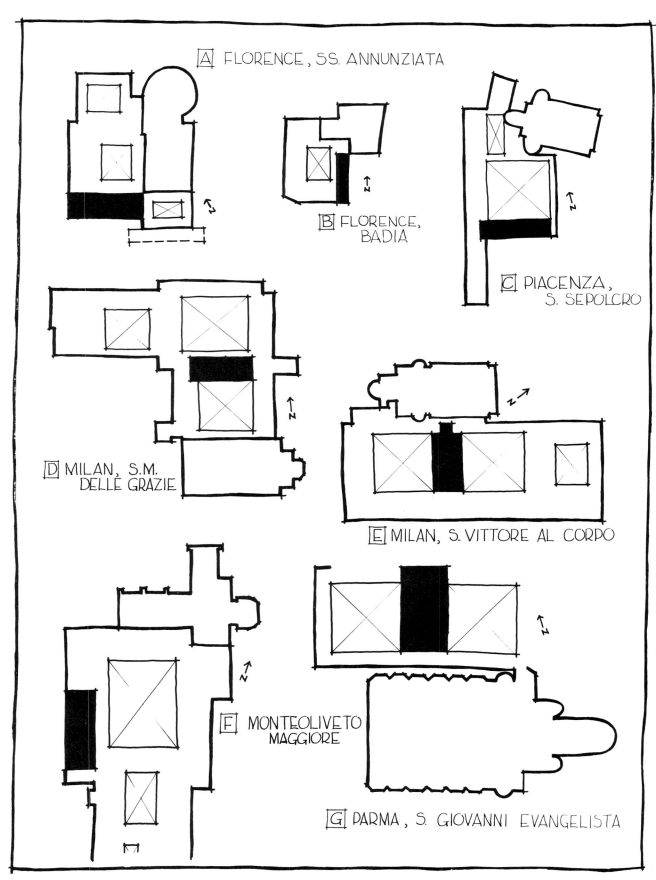

A FLORENCE, SS. ANNUNZIATA

B FLORENCE, BADIA

C PIACENZA, S. SEPOLCRO

D MILAN, S.M. DELLE GRAZIE

E MILAN, S. VITTORE AL CORPO

F MONTEOLIVETO MAGGIORE

G PARMA, S. GIOVANNI EVANGELISTA

13. Diagrammatic plans of seven Italian monasteries of the fifteenth and early sixteenth centuries showing position of libraries (in black) on second floor. No common scale (author).

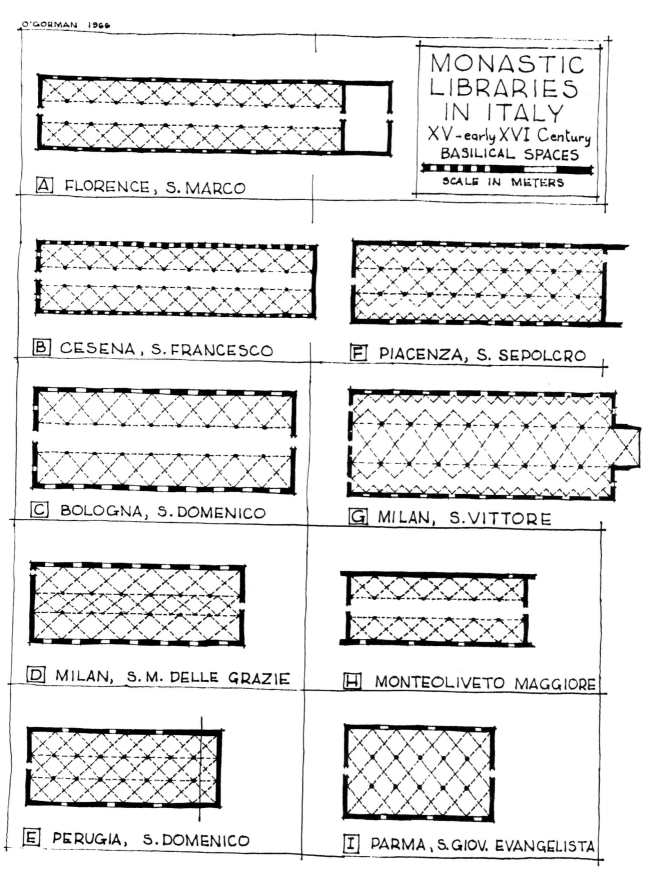

MONASTIC LIBRARIES IN ITALY
XV - early XVI Century
BASILICAL SPACES

SCALE IN METERS

A FLORENCE, S. MARCO

B CESENA, S. FRANCESCO

F PIACENZA, S. SEPOLCRO

C BOLOGNA, S. DOMENICO

G MILAN, S. VITTORE

D MILAN, S.M. DELLE GRAZIE

H MONTEOLIVETO MAGGIORE

E PERUGIA, S. DOMENICO

I PARMA, S. GIOV. EVANGELISTA

14. Plans of nine monastic libraries of the fifteenth and early sixteenth centuries (author).

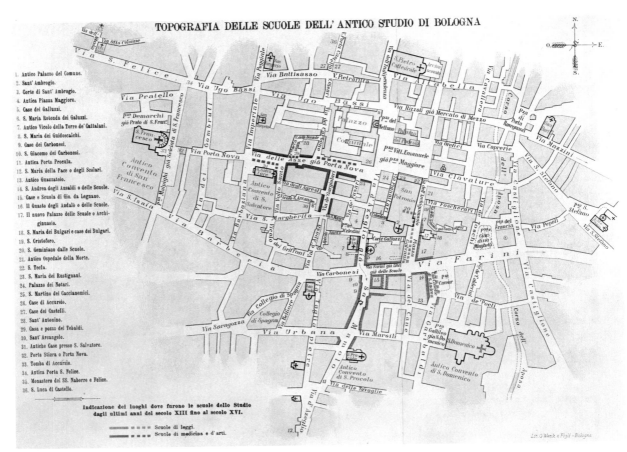

15. Bologna. Plan of center city showing distribution of the *scuole* of the University from the thirteenth to the sixteenth century (after F. Cavazza, *Le scuole dell'antico studio bolognese*, Milan, 1896).

16. Bologna, S. Domenico. Aerial View, showing library between cloisters (photo: A. Villani).

17. Bologna, S. Domenico. Area beneath library (photo: A. Villani).

18. Bologna, S. Domenico. Library wing, exterior (photo: A. Villani).

19. Bologna, S. Domenico. Library, interior (photo: A. Villani).

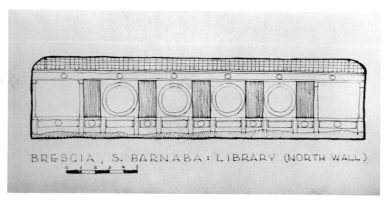

20. Brescia, S. Barnaba. Library, north wall showing architectonic organization of frescoes (author).

1. Rome, Ancient library on Esquiline. Interior elevation, detail (after Clark, *Care of Books*).

22. Brescia, S. Barnaba. Library, interior (photo: Direzione Musei e Pinacoteca, Brescia).

23. Brescia, S. Barnaba. Library, exterior (photo: Jean Baer O'Gorman).

24. Cesena, S. Francesco. Library, interior (photo: Alinari).

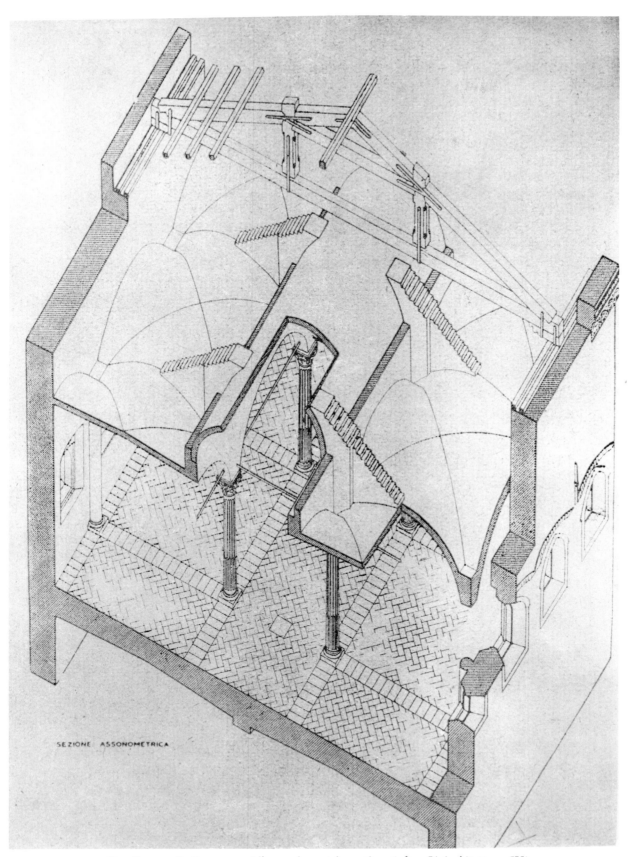

SEZIONE ASSONOMETRICA

25. Cesena, S. Francesco, Library, isometric section (after *L'Architettura,* IV).

26. Cesena, S. Francesco. Library, exterior (center), with window of former church to right (photo: Jean Baer O'Gorman).

27. Cesena, S. Francesco. Library, detail of reading desks (after Clark, *Care of Books*).

28. Cesena, S. Francesco. Library, exterior (photo: G. Zangheri).

29. Fra Bartolomeo, *View of SS. Annunziata* (detail), shortly after 1500. Library in center (Florence, Uffizi 45P) (Gabinetto Fotografico della Soprintendenza alle Gallerie, Florence).

30. R. Ghirlandaio, *View of SS. Annunziata,* 1514, showing library to left (detail of *Annunciation,* Cappella dei Priori, Palazzo Vecchio, Florence) (after C. Ricci, *Il Tempio malatestiano,* Milan-Rome [1924]).

31. Florence, SS. Annunziata. Chiostro Grande (former library to left) (photo: G. Giusti).

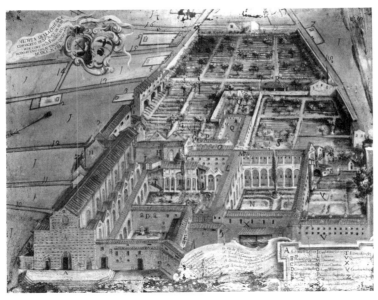

32. *Veduta della chiesa e del convento di S. Croce,* 1718, showing library between cloisters (Museo dell'opera di S. Croce, Florence) (photo: Alinari).

33. Florence, S. Croce. Library from second cloister (photo: Jean Baer O'Gorman).

34. Florence, S. Croce. Second cloister in flood, November, 1966 (photo: P. L. Brunetti).

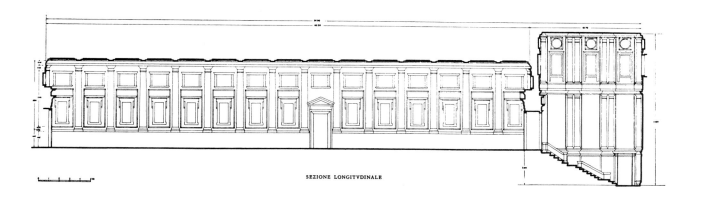

SEZIONE LONGITVDINALE

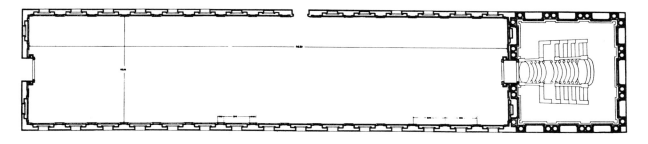

PIANTA

35. Florence, S. Lorenzo. Plan and section of library (after B. Apollonj, *Le opere architettoniche di Michelangelo a Firenze,* Rome, 1934).

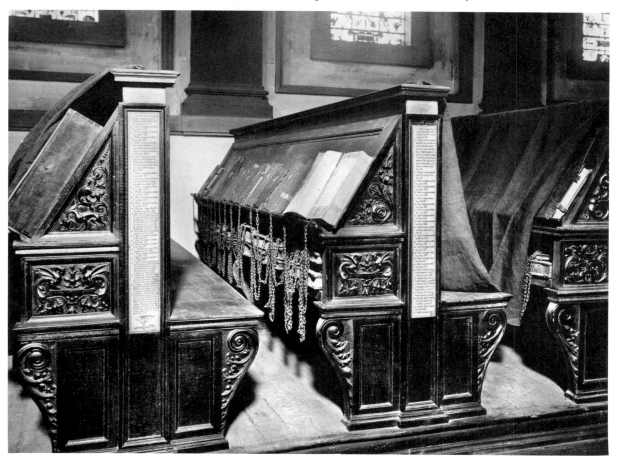

36. Florence, S. Lorenzo. Library detail of interior (photo: Alinari).

37. Florence, S. Lorenzo. Library, interior (photo: Alinari).

38. Florence, S. Marco. Library, interior (photo: Gabinetto Fotografico della Soprintendenza alle Gallerie, Florence).

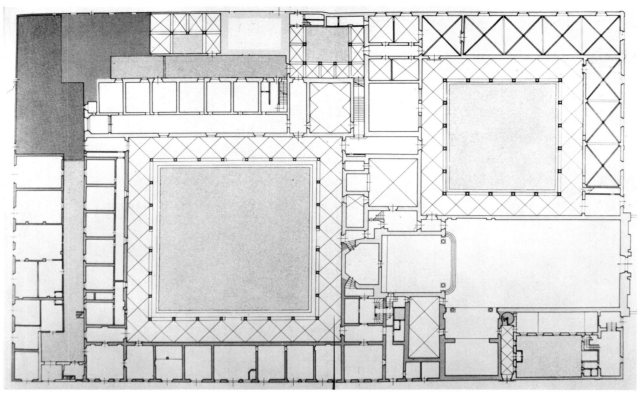

39. Florence, S. Marco. Ground floor plan (after *Architetti*, IV).

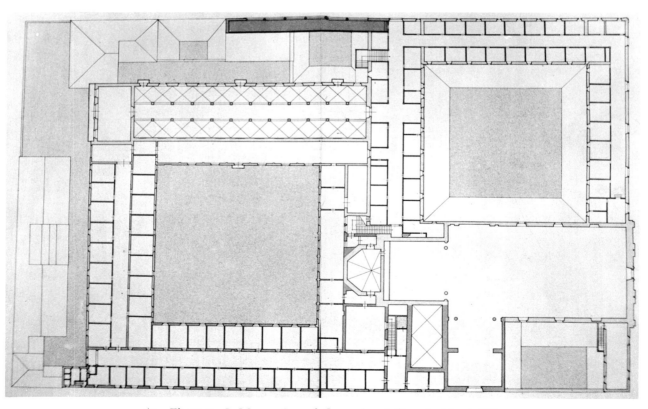

40. Florence, S. Marco. Second floor plan (after *Architetti*, IV).

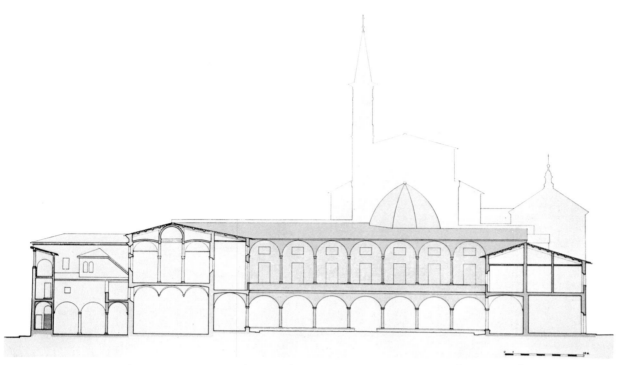

41. Florence, S. Marco. Cloister of S. Domenico, section with library to left
(after *Architetti,* IV).

42. Giovanni Antonio Sogliani, *View of S. Marco,* 1536,
showing library to left (detail of *Crucifixion,* large
refectory, S. Marco, Florence) (photo: Alinari).

43. Florence, S. Marco. Dormitory, interior
(photo: Alinari).

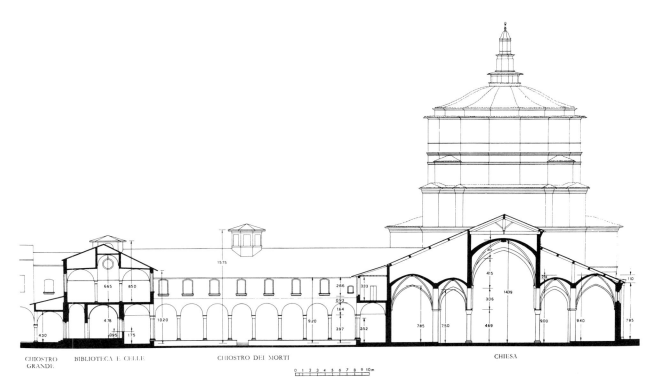

44. Milan, S. Maria delle Grazie. Chiostro dei Morti, section with library to left (after A. Pica, *Il Gruppo monumentale di S. Maria delle Grazie in Milano,* Rome, 1937).

45. Milan, S. Maria delle Grazie. Library, longitudinal section (after Pica, *Gruppo monumentale*).

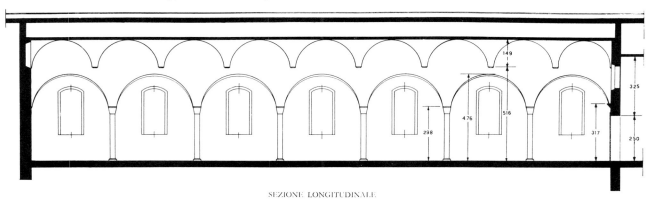

46. Milan, S. Vittore al Corpo. Dormitory corridor (photo: Museo Nazionale Scienza e
Tecnica, Milan).

47. Milan, S. Vittore al Corpo. Cloister
with library to left center (photo:
Museo Nazionale Scienza e Tecnica).

48. Milan, S. Vittore al Corpo. Library, interior (photo: Museo Nazionale
Scienza e Tecnica).

49. Monteoliveto Maggiore. Library, interior (photo: Alinari).

50. Padua, S. Giovanni di Verdara. Library, interior (photo: Courtesy Lionello Puppi).

51. Parma, S. Giovanni Evangelista. Library, interior (photo Jean Baer O'Gorman).

52. Parma, S. Giovanni Evangelista. Library, exterior (photo: Jean Baer O'Gorman).

53. Perugia, S. Domenico. Library, interior (after *Miscellanea di scritti vari in memoria di Alfonso Gallo,* Florence, 1956).

54. Perugia, S. Domenico. Library, exterior (photo: Jean Baer O'Gorman).

55. Piacenza, S. Sepolcro. Library, interior (photo: Jean Baer O'Gorman).

56. Piacenza, S. Sepolcro. Library, diagrammatic section (author).

57. Piacenza, S. Sepolcro. Library, exterior (photo: Jean Baer O'Gorman).

58. Venice, S. Giorgia Maggiore. Aerial view with presumed library perpendicular to church (Jacopo de' Barbieri, 1500).

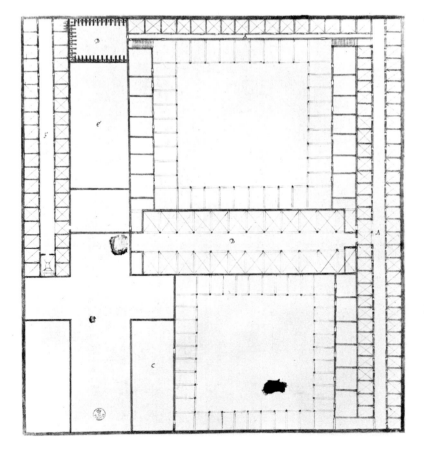

59. Giorgio Vasari il Giovane. Plan of second floor of a monastery, 1598 (from Città Ideale; Florence, Uffizi 4544A) (Gabinetto Fotografico della Soprintendenza alle Gallerie, Florence).

60. Vicenza, S. Corona. Library, two views of interior (photo: courtesy
S. Zanarotti).